Wasted Lives

WASTED LIVES

Modernity and its Outcasts

Zygmunt Bauman

polity

First published in 2004 by Polity Press in association with Blackwell Publishing Ltd.

Reprinted 2004, 2005, 2006, 2008

Polity Press
65 Bridge Street
Cambridge CB2 1UR, UK

Polity Press
350 Main Street
Malden, MA 02148, USA

ISBN: 978-0-7456-3164-6
ISBN: 978-0-7456-3165-3 (pb)

A catalogue record for this book is available from the British Library and has been applied for from the Library of Congress.

Typeset in 11 on 13 pt Berling
by SNP Best-set Typesetter Ltd., Hong Kong
Printed and bound in the United States by Odyssey Press Inc., Gonic, New Hampshire

For further information on Polity, visit our website: www.polity.co.uk

Contents

Acknowledgements   vi

Introduction   1

1   **In the beginning was design**
    Or the waste of order-building   9

2   **Are there too many of them?**
    Or the waste of economic progress   34

3   **To each waste its dumping site**
    Or the waste of globalization   63

4   **Culture of waste**   94

Notes   134

Acknowledgements

My thanks go, as so many times in the past, to John Thompson for his spot-on critical insights and priceless advice, and to Ann Bone for the loving care and exemplary patience with which she spots and corrects the author's errors and removes the traces of his slackness and negligence.

Introduction

There is more than one way in which the story of modernity (or any story for that matter) can be told. This book is one of such stories.

Talking of Aglaura, one of the bizarre yet eerily familiar cities listed in *Le città invisibili*, Italo Calvino's Marco Polo said that he could hardly go 'beyond the things its own inhabitants have always repeated', even if their stories jarred with what he himself thought he was looking at. 'You would like to say what it is, but everything previously said of Aglaura imprisons your words and obliges you to repeat rather than say.' And so, securely ensconced within the city walls made of the ever repeated stories after the fashion in which the ramparts of some cities are made of stones, Aglaurians 'live in an Aglaura which grows only with the name Aglaura and they do not notice the Aglaura that grows on the ground'. How could they, indeed, behave differently? After all, 'the city they speak of has much of what is needed to exist, whereas the city that exists on its site, exists less.'[1]

The residents of Leonia, another of Calvino's *Invisible Cities*, would say, if asked, that their passion is 'the enjoyment of new and different things'. Indeed, each morning they 'wear brand-new clothing, take from the latest model refrigerator still unopened tins, listening to the last-minute jingles from the most up-to-date radio'. But each morning 'the remains of yesterday's Leonia await the garbage truck' and a stranger like Marco Polo, looking, so to speak, through the cracks in Leonia's story-walls, would wonder whether the Leonians' true passion is not instead 'the joy of expelling, discarding, cleansing themselves of a recurrent impurity'. Why otherwise would street cleaners be 'welcomed like angels', even if their mission is 'surrounded by respectful silence', and understandably so – 'once things have been cast off nobody wants to have to think about them further.' As the Leonians excel in their chase after novelties, 'a fortress of indestructible leftovers' surrounds the city, 'dominating it on every side, like a chain of mountains'.

Do the Leonians see those mountains, you may ask? Sometimes they might, particularly when a freak gust of wind wafts into their spick'n'span homes a stench reminiscent of a rubbish heap rather than of the all-fresh, all-glittering, all-fragrant innards of novelty shops. Once that has happened, it is hard for them to avert their eyes; they would have to look worriedly, with fear and trembling, at the mountains – and be horrified by what they saw. They would abhor the mountains' ugliness and detest them for blotting the landscape – for being foul, unsavoury, offending and altogether revolting, for harbouring dangers they know and dangers unlike anything they knew before, for stocking the hazards they can see and such hazards as they can't even guess. They would not like what they saw, and they wouldn't want to look at it any longer. They would hate the leftovers of their yesterday's reveries as passionately as they loved the brand-new dresses and up-to-the-minute toys. They would wish the mountains away, would want them to disappear – to be dynamited, crushed, pulverized or dissolved. They would complain against the sloth of the street cleaners, leniency of foremen and complacency of bosses.

Even more than the leftovers themselves the Leonians would abhor the idea of their indestructibility. They would be horror-stricken by the news that the mountains they keenly wish away are reluctant to degrade, deteriorate and decompose on their own, as well as being resistant, nay immune, to solvents. Hoping against hope, they wouldn't take in the simple truth that the odious heaps of waste can only *not be* if they have not been *made to be* (by them, the Leonians!) in the first place. They would refuse to accept that (as Marco Polo's message goes, which Leonians would not hear) 'as the city renews every day, it preserves all of itself in its only definitive form: yesterday's sweepings piled up on the sweepings of the day before yesterday and of all its days and years and decades.' Leonians would not listen to Marco Polo's message since what the message would tell them (were they willing to hear it, that is) was that rather than preserving what they claim to love and desire, they only manage to make the rubbish permanent. Only the useless, the off-putting, the repellent, the poisonous and the frightening is tough enough to be still there as the time passes.

Following the Aglaurians' example, Leonians live daily, we may say, in a Leonia which 'grows only with the name Leonia', blissfully unaware of that other Leonia which grows on the ground. At least they avert or shut their eyes, trying hard not to see it. Exactly as in the Aglaurian case, the city they speak of 'has much of what they need to exist'. Most importantly, it contains the story of the passion for novelty which they go on repeating daily so that the passion they speak of can forever be born again and replenished and the story of that passion could go on being told, heard, avidly listened to and staunchly believed.

It takes a stranger like Marco Polo to ask: what in the end is the Leonians' staple product? The enchanting, brand new things, enticingly fresh and seductively mysterious, since virgin and untried – or rather the ever rising mounds of waste? How, for instance, is their passion for fashion to be explained? What, indeed, is that fashion about – is it about substituting more beautiful things for things less adorable, or about the joy felt when things are thrown on the rubbish heap after first being stripped of their glamour and allure? Are things thrown away because of their ugliness, or are they ugly because they have been earmarked for the tip?

Tricky questions, indeed. Answering them is no less tricky a task. The answers would depend on stories echoing between the walls that rose out of the memories of the stories told, repeated, listened to, ingested and absorbed.

Were the questions to be addressed to a Leonian, the answers would be that more and more new and newer things must be produced to replace other things that are less prepossessing or useful or have lost their use. But if you ask Marco Polo, a traveller, a sceptical stranger, an uninvolved outsider, a baffled newcomer – he would answer that in Leonia things are declared useless and promptly thrown away because other, new and improved objects of desire beckon, and that they are bound to be thrown away to make room for such newer things. He would answer that in Leonia it is today's novelty that makes yesterday's novelty obsolete and destined for the rubbish heap. Both answers ring true; both seem to convey the Leonians' life story. So in the end the choice depends on whether one story is being monotonously repeated or, on the contrary, thoughts are roaming free in the space free of stories . . .

Ivan Klima remembers dining with the President of the Ford company in his residence in Detroit. The guest asked the host, who boasted of the rising number of spanking new Ford cars leaving the assembly line, 'how he removed all those cars from the world once they'd reached the end of their service'. 'He replied that this was no problem. Anything that was manufactured could vanish without trace, it was merely a technical problem. And he smiled at the thought of a totally empty, cleansed world.'

After the dinner, Klima went to see how that 'technical problem' was dealt with. Used cars, cars declared used up and so no longer wanted, were squeezed by gigantic presses into neat metal boxes. 'But those metal boxes did not vanish from the world . . . They probably melt down the crushed metal to make iron and new steel for new cars, and thus rubbish is transformed into new rubbish, only slightly increased in quantity.'

Having heard the story and seen what it was allegedly reporting, Klima muses: 'No, this isn't a mere technical problem. Because the spirit of dead things rises over the earth and over the waters, and its breath forebodes evil.'[2]

This book is devoted to that 'not a mere technical problem'. It tries to explain what else it is in addition to being technical, and why it is a problem in the first place.

Our planet is full.

This is, let me make myself clear, not a statement in physical or even human geography. In terms of physical space and the spread of human cohabitation, the planet is anything but full. On the contrary, the total size of sparsely populated or depopulated lands viewed as uninhabitable and incapable of supporting human life seems to be expanding rather than shrinking. As *technological* progress offers (at a rising cost, to be sure) new means of survival in habitats that were previously deemed unfit for human settlement, it also erodes the ability of many habitats to sustain the populations they previously used to accommodate and feed. Meanwhile *economic* progress renders once effective modes of making a living unviable and impracticable, thereby adding to the size of the wastelands laying fallow and abandoned.

'The planet is full' is a statement *in sociology and political science*. It refers not to the state of the earth, but to the ways and means of its inhabitants. It signals the disappearance of 'no man's lands', territories fit to be defined and/or treated as void of human habitation as well as devoid of sovereign administration – and thus open to (clamouring for!) colonization and settlement. Such territories, now largely absent, for a greater part of modern history played the crucial role of dumping grounds for the human waste turned out in ever rising volumes in the parts of the globe affected by the processes of 'modernization'.

The production of 'human waste', or more correctly wasted humans (the 'excessive' and 'redundant', that is the population of those who either could not or were not wished to be recognized or allowed to stay), is an inevitable outcome of modernization, and an inseparable accompaniment of modernity. It is an inescapable side-effect of *order-building* (each order casts some parts of the extant population as 'out of place', 'unfit' or 'undesirable') and of *economic progress* (that cannot proceed without degrading and devaluing the previously effective modes of 'making a living' and therefore cannot but deprive their practitioners of their livelihood).

For a greater part of modern history, however, huge parts of the globe ('backward', 'underdeveloped' parts, when measured by the ambitions of the already modern, that is obsessively modernizing, sector of the planet) stayed wholly or partly unaffected by modernizing pressures, thus escaping their 'overpopulation' effect. Confronted with the modernizing niches of the globe, such ('premodern', 'underdeveloped') parts tended to be viewed and treated as lands able to absorb the excess of the population of the 'developed countries'; natural destinations for the export of 'redundant humans' and obvious, ready-made dumping sites for the human waste of modernization. The disposal of human waste produced in the 'modernized' and still 'modernizing' parts of the globe was the deepest meaning of colonization and imperialist conquests – both made possible, and in fact inevitable, by the power differential continuously reproduced by the stark inequality of 'development' (euphemistically called 'cultural lag'), resulting in turn from the confinement of the modern fashion of life to a 'privileged' section of the planet. That inequality allowed the modern part of the globe to seek, and find, *global* solutions to *locally* produced 'overpopulation' problems.

This situation could last as long as modernity (that is, a perpetual, compulsive, obsessive and addictive *modernization*) remained a privilege. Once modernity turned, as it was intended and bound to, into the universal condition of humankind, the effects of its planetary dominion have come home to roost. As the triumphant progress of modernization has reached the furthest lands of the planet and practically the totality of human production and consumption has become money and market mediated, and the processes of the commodification, commercialization and monetarization of human livelihoods have penetrated every nook and cranny of the globe, global solutions to locally produced problems, or global outlets for local excesses, are no longer available. Just the contrary is the case: all localities (including, most notably, the highly modernized ones) have to bear the consequences of modernity's global triumph. They are now faced with the need to seek (in vain, it seems) *local* solutions to *globally* produced problems.

To cut the long story short: the new fullness of the planet means, essentially, *an acute crisis of the human waste disposal industry*. While the production of human waste goes on unabated and rises to new heights, the planet is fast running short of refuse dumps and the tools of waste recycling.

As if to make the already troublesome state of affairs even more complex and threatening, a new powerful source of 'wasted humans' has been added to the original two. Globalization has become the third, and currently the most prolific and least controlled, 'production line' of human waste or wasted humans. It has also put a new gloss on the old problem and imbued it with an altogether new significance and unprecedented urgency.

The global spread of the modern form of life set loose and put in motion enormous and constantly rising quantities of human beings bereaved of their heretofore adequate ways and means of survival in both the biological and social/cultural sense of that notion. For the resulting population pressures, the old familiar colonialist pressures but reversed in direction, there are no readily available outlets – either for 'recycling' or for safe 'disposal'. Hence the alarms about the overpopulation of the globe; hence also the new centrality of 'immigrant' and 'asylum seeker' problems to the contemporary political agenda and the rising role played by vague and diffuse 'security fears' in the emergent global strategies and the logic of power struggles.

The essentially elemental, unregulated and politically uncontrolled nature of globalization processes has resulted in the establishment of 'frontier-land' conditions of a new sort in the planetary 'space of flows' to which a great part of the power capacity once lodged in the sovereign modern states has been transferred. The brittle and incurably precarious equilibrium of frontier-land settings rests notoriously on 'mutually assured vulnerability'. Hence the alarms about deteriorating security which magnify the already plentiful supplies of 'security fears' while simultaneously shifting public concerns and the outlets for individual anxiety away from the economic and social roots of trouble and towards concerns for personal (bodily) safety. In its turn, the thriving 'security industry' rapidly becomes one of the principal branches of waste production and the paramount factor in the waste disposal problem.

This is, in the broadest of outlines, the setting for contemporary life. The 'problems of (human) waste and (human) waste disposal' weigh ever more heavily on the liquid modern, consumerist culture of individualization. They saturate all the most important sectors of social life, tending to dominate life strategies and colour the most important life activities, prompting them to generate their own *sui generis* waste: stillborn, unfit, invalid or unviable human relationships, born with the mark of impending wastage.

These issues, and some of their derivatives, are the major themes of this book. Their analysis here is preliminary. My major, perhaps even only, concern is to offer an alternative viewpoint from which stock can be taken of those aspects of modern life that recent developments have drawn out of their previous concealment and brought into the limelight, allowing certain facets of the contemporary world to be better seen and their logic better understood. This book ought to be read as an invitation to take another, and somewhat different look at the allegedly all-too-familiar modern world we all share and inhabit.

1

In the beginning was design

Or the waste of order-building

There was a time, of course, when the five of us did not know one another . . . We still don't know one another, but what is possible and can be tolerated by the five of us is not possible and cannot be tolerated with the sixth one. In any case, we are five and don't want to be six . . .

Long explanations would almost amount to accepting him in our circle, so we prefer not to explain and not to accept him . . .

Franz Kafka, 'Fellowship'

According to a recent report by the Joseph Rowntree Foundation,

The number of young people battling depression has doubled in twelve years, as hundreds of thousands find themselves excluded from rising levels of education and prosperity . . . When those born in 1958 completed a questionnaire on their mental health in 1981, 7 per cent had a tendency to non-clinical depression. The equivalent figure for the 1970 cohort, interviewed in 1996, was 14 per cent. Analysis suggested that the rise was linked to the younger group having grown up with more experience of unemployment. Those with a degree were a third less likely to be depressed.[1]

Depression is a most unpleasant, harrowing and incapacitating mental condition, but as this and numerous other reports suggest, it is not the only symptom of the malaise that haunts the new generation born into the brave new liquid modern world – whereas it did not seem to affect, at least not to the same extent, their immediate predecessors. 'More experience of unemployment', however traumatic and painful it undoubtedly is, does not seem to be the sole cause of the malaise.

The so-called 'Generation X' of young men and women born in the 1970s, in Britain or other 'developed' countries, knows ailments of which older generations were unaware; not necessarily more ailments, or ailments that are more acute, distressing and mortifying, but ones that are distinctly different, novel – one could say 'specifically liquid modern' maladies and afflictions. And it has novel reasons (some replacing, some added to the traditional ones) to feel ruffled, disturbed and often aggrieved – even if the analysts and the appointed healers, following the natural inclinations we all share, resort matter-of-factly to the diagnoses they remember best and to the cures that were most widely applied at the time they were trained to seek and recommend them.

One of the diagnoses most commonly on offer is unemployment, and particularly the poor job prospects for the school-leavers who enter fresh on a market concerned with raising profits through cutting labour costs and asset-stripping rather than creating new jobs and building new assets. One of the cures most widely pondered is state subsidies that would make the hiring of youngsters a good business (for as long as the subsidies last). One of the most commonly offered recommendations to the young meanwhile is to be flexible and not particularly choosy, not to expect too much from jobs, to take the jobs as they come without asking too many questions, and to treat them as an opportunity to be enjoyed on the spot as long as it lasts rather than as an introductory chapter of a 'life project', a matter of self-esteem and self-definition, or a warrant of long-term security.

Comfortingly, therefore, the package-idea of 'unemployment' entails the diagnosis of the trouble complete with the best available cure and a list of straightforward and reassuringly obvious routines to be followed on the way to convalescence. The prefix 'un' suggests anomaly; '*un*employment' is a name for a manifestly temporary and *abnormal* condition and so the nature of the complaint is patently transient and curable. The notion of 'unemployment' inherits its semantic load from the self-awareness of a society which used to cast its members as producers first and last, and which also believed in full employment as not just a desirable and attainable social condition but also its own ultimate destination; a society which therefore cast employment as a key – *the* key – to the resolution of the issues of, simultaneously, socially acceptable personal identity, secure social position, individual and collective survival, social order and systemic reproduction.

The human world, as Siegfried Kracauer aptly expressed it, is saturated with *Sollen* ('shoulds') – the sort of ideas that 'want to become reality themselves': they 'have an inborn drive to realize themselves'. Such ideas 'take in sociological significance' once they 'begin to have an effect on social world'[2] – as they struggle for it, keenly though with mixed success. Modern history stood out from the preceding stretches of human history by laying its 'shoulds' open, making them explicit and resolving to 'live towards them'. Modernity, to borrow from Kracauer again, carried on a 'double existence', orienting itself 'toward the Beyond in which everything in the Here would find its meaning and conclusion'.[3]

Of such 'shoulds' there was never a shortage; modern history was a prolific factory of 'good society' models. The most ideologically inspired among the battles with which modern history was strewn were waged on the Sollen front lines, between furiously competitive 'shoulds'. And yet all varieties of the 'should' agreed that the litmus test of a 'good society' was workplaces for all and a productive role for anyone. Modern history, endemically critical of every present as stopping far too short of the 'ought', proceeded through fighting many ills and villains, but the decisive battle was deemed to be fought against the dearth of workplaces and an insufficient supply of productive roles or of the will to take them up.

How different is the idea of 'redundancy' that has shot into prominence during the lifetime of Generation X! Where the prefix 'un' in 'unemployment' used to suggest a departure from the norm – as in 'unhealthy' or 'unwell' – there is no such suggestion in the notion of 'redundancy'. No inkling of abnormality, anomaly, spell of ill-health or a momentary slip. 'Redundancy' whispers permanence and hints at the ordinariness of the condition. It names a condition without offering a ready-to-use antonym. It suggests a new shape of current normality and

the shape of things that are imminent and bound to stay as they
are.

To be 'redundant' means to be supernumerary, unneeded, of no
use – whatever the needs and uses are that set the standard of
usefulness and indispensability. The others do not need you; they
can do as well, and better, without you. There is no self-evident
reason for your being around and no obvious justification for your
claim to the right to stay around. To be declared redundant means
to have been disposed of *because of being disposable* – just like the
empty and non-refundable plastic bottle or once-used syringe,
an unattractive commodity with no buyers, or a substandard or
stained product without use thrown off the assembly line by the
quality inspectors. 'Redundancy' shares its semantic space with
'rejects', 'wastrels', 'garbage', 'refuse' – with *waste*. The destination
of the *unemployed*, of the 'reserve army of labour', was to be
called back into active service. The destination of waste is the
waste-yard, the rubbish heap.

More often than not, indeed routinely, people declared 'redundant' are talked about as mainly a financial problem. They need
to be 'provided for' – that is fed, shod and sheltered. They would
not survive on their own – they lack the 'means of survival'
(meaning mostly biological survival, the opposite of a death from
malnutrition or exposure). The answer to redundancy is as financial as the definition of the problem: state-provided, state-
legislated, state-endorsed or state-promoted and means-tested
handouts (variously, but always euphemistically, dubbed welfare
benefits, tax credits, reliefs, grants, allowances). Those unsympa-
thetic to such an answer tend to contest it in similarly financial
terms (under the heading 'can we afford it?') – for the 'financial
burden' all such measures impose on the taxpayers.

The need to assist the survival of people declared 'redundant',
perhaps to assist it permanently (that is, to put it bluntly, the need
to accept the right of a permanently and incurably redundant part
of the population to a measure of wealth they neither help to
produce nor are needed to produce), is however only some of the
problem the jobless present to themselves and to others. Another,
much more seminal – though anything but properly acknowledged and addressed – part of the problem is that in the section

of the world commonly caught by the idea of 'society' there is no compartment reserved for 'human waste' (more to the point, wasted humans). Even if the threat hanging over *biological* survival is dealt with and fought back against effectively, such a no-mean feat would come nowhere near the assurance of *social* survival. It will not be sufficient for a readmission of the 'redundant' to the society from which they have been excluded – just as storing industrial waste in refrigerated containers would hardly suffice to make it into a market commodity.

A feeling that redundancy may signal such 'social homelessness', with all the attendant loss of self-esteem and life purpose, or a suspicion that it may at any moment become their lot even if it has not yet, is the part of the life experience of Generation X that it does not share with the preceding generations, however acute and resented the misery of those generations might have been. Indeed, Generation X has ample reasons to be depressed. Unwelcome, tolerated at best, cast firmly on the receiving side of socially recommended or tolerated action, treated in the best of cases as an object of benevolence, charity and pity (challenged, to rub salt into the wound, as undeserved) but not of brotherly help, charged with indolence and suspected of iniquitous intentions and criminal inclinations, it has few reasons to treat 'society' as a home to which one owes loyalty and concern. As Danièle Linhart, co-author of the *Perte d'emploi, perte de soi*,[4] suggests, 'these men and women lose not only their jobs, their projects, their orientation points, the confidence of being in control of their lives; they also find themselves stripped of their dignity as workers, of self-esteem, of the feeling of being useful and having a social place of their own.'[5] So why should the suddenly disqualified employees respect the rules of the political-democratic game if those of the world of labour are blatantly ignored?

Wretched and miserable the unemployed in the *society of producers* (including those temporarily 'away from the production line') might have been, but their place in society was unquestionable and secure. On the battlefront of production, who would deny the need for strong reserve units ready for the fray if the need arose? The unfulfilled consumers in the *society of consumers* cannot be so sure. One thing they can be certain of is that having been cast out of the only game in town, they are no longer players – and so no longer needed. Once, to be a would-be producer it was enough to fulfil the conditions set for admission to the company of producers. A promise to be a diligent consumer and laying claim to the status of consumer will not suffice, though, for admission to the company of consumers. The society of consumers has no room for flawed, incomplete, unfulfilled consumers. In Samuel Butler's *Erewhon* it was 'ill luck of any kind, or even ill treatment at the hands of others' that was 'considered an offence against society, inasmuch as it [made] people uncomfortable to hear of it'. 'Loss of fortune, therefore' was 'punished hardly less severely than physical delinquency'.[6] Flawed consumers would not know when they might be declared criminals.

Generation X is also more sharply polarized than the immediately preceding generation, and the dividing line has been moved up the social hierarchy. It is true that the perplexing volatility of social placement, the dimness of prospects, the living from hand to mouth with no reliable chance of a durable, or at least a longer term settlement, the vagueness of the rules that need to be learned and mastered in order to get by – these haunt them all without discrimination, breeding anxiety in everyone, stripping all or almost all members of the generation of their self-assurance and self-esteem. The lower threshold of effective therapy against all such afflictions has been lifted, however, beyond the reach of the great majority. It is now a higher education degree that has become the minimal condition of hope for even a sporting chance of a dignified and secure life (which does not mean that a degree vouchsafes a smooth ride; it only appears to do that because it remains a minority privilege). The world, it seems, has made another leap, and yet more of its residents, unable to bear the speed, have fallen off the accelerating vehicle – while more of those not yet inside have failed to make the running, to catch up, and jump in.

The worries of the X generation – redundancy worries – differ from the troubles lived with and recorded by the previous generations. They are also suffered and tackled in their own distinct and unique way. And yet they are not unprecedented.

Since the beginning of modern times each successive generation has had its shipwrecks marooned in the social void: the 'collateral casualties' of progress. While many managed to jump onto
the speeding vehicle and thoroughly enjoyed the ride, many others
– less cunning, adroit, clever, muscular or adventurous – lagged
behind or were barred entry to the overcrowded carriage, if they
weren't crushed under its wheels. In the vehicle of progress, the
numbers of seats and standing places did not as a rule suffice to
accommodate all the willing passengers and admission was at all
times selective; this is perhaps why the dream of joining the ride
was, for so many, a sweet one. Progress was advertised under the
slogan of more happiness for *more* people; but perhaps the need
for *fewer* (and ever fewer) people to keep on the move, to accelerate and to climb those heights that once would have required a
much larger crowd to negotiate, invade and conquer was what
progress, the trade mark of the modern era, was in the last instance
about.

In this respect the Generation X is not the first to have good
reasons to be depressed. What makes its predicament peculiar
however is, to start with, the fact that an unusually large part of
the cohort has, or feels as if it has, gone by the board and been
left behind. Peculiar also is the widespread feeling of confusion,
puzzlement and perplexity. All similarities notwithstanding, our
contemporaries feel intuitively that the present trouble is unlike
the troubles of past generations, even though they too had their
full measure of misery. Most importantly perhaps, nowadays we
tend to feel that the patented medicine inherited from the past
does not work any more. However adept we may be in the arts
of crisis management, we do not really know how to tackle this
trouble. We lack perhaps even the tools to think about reasonable
ways of tackling it.

Societies of our parents and grandparents also set their conditions for admission and for the issue of residence permits. Their
conditions, however, were spelled out clearly, with no mistake
about their terms, and came complete with similarly clear instructions on how to proceed to meet them. Those societies laid their
career-and-tenure tracks to start just on the other side of each
entry point. The tracks were mostly narrow, leaving little elbow

room and holding even less promise of adventure, and so might have appeared intimidating and unbearably constraining to those for whom security and certainty were not an issue. (Sigmund Freud famously reprocessed their torments into a general theory of the discontents and psychological disorders which civilization was bound to breed.) But to those still in need of a trustworthy boat that promised safe passage, the destination was neither a mystery nor a matter of agonizing choice; the tasks of navigation were not beset with uncountable and unaccountable risks. What was left to those wielding the oars was to paddle diligently and assiduously, following the ship's rules 'to the letter'.

Today's troubles have changed: they are *goal-related* rather than *means-bound*. The routines of yore, vilified and resented by so many while they were still in full force, have by now died out – taking that security-inspiring trust with them into the grave. Now it is no longer a question of finding the means to clearly defined ends and then holding them fast and using them with a maximum of skill and to the greatest effect. It is now a question of the elusiveness (and all too often delusiveness) of ends – fading and dissolving quicker than the time it takes to reach them, unfixed, unreliable and commonly seen as unworthy of undying commitment and dedication. The rules of admission to the set tracks and the permits to embark on them can no longer be relied on either. If they have not vanished altogether, they tend to be withdrawn and replaced without notice. Most importantly, for anyone who is once excluded and assigned to waste there are no obvious return paths to a fully fledged membership. Nor are there any alternative, officially endorsed and mapped roads one could follow (or, for that matter, be forced to follow) towards an alternative title of belonging.

The crucial point is that while all this happens on our doorsteps, we cannot honestly tell what we, using our homemade tools and home-grown resources, can do to avert the bane. It is no longer a question of a temporary hiccup, of a slowdown that follows an overheating of the economy and precedes another boom, a temporary irritant that will go away and 'become history' once we tinker a bit with the taxes, subsidies, allowances and incentives stimulating another 'consumer-led recovery'. The roots of the trouble, it seems, have moved further away than we can reach. And their most dense and thick clusters are not to be found on any of the Ordnance Survey maps.

Excursus: *On telling stories*   Stories are like searchlights and spotlights; they brighten up parts of the stage while leaving the rest in darkness. Were they to illuminate the whole of the stage evenly, they would not really be of use. Their task, after all, is to 'cure' the stage, making it ready for the viewers' visual and intellectual consumption; to create a picture one can absorb, comprehend and retain out of the anarchy of blots and stains one can neither take in nor make sense of.

Stories aid the seekers of comprehension by separating the relevant from the irrelevant, actions from their settings, the plot from its background, and the heroes or the villains at the centre of the plot from the hosts of supernumeraries and dummies. It is the mission of stories to select, and it is in their nature to include through exclusion and to illuminate through casting shadows. It is a grave misunderstanding, and injustice, to blame stories for favouring one part of the stage while neglecting another. Without selection there would be no story. To say 'this would be a fine story if only it did not skip this or that' is like saying 'these would be fine windows for seeing through the walls if they were not framed and kept apart by the walls between them.'

As if anticipating the impending disavowal of modernity's delusive hopes, Jorge Luis Borges penned the story of Ireneo Funes, who as a boy was thrown from a horse and left crippled and 'virtually incapable of general, platonic ideas' (that is, of abstracting: of putting certain aspects of what he saw in focus by leaving the rest out). Instead he was able to (had to!) perceive 'every grape that had been pressed into the wine and all the stalks and tendrils of its vineyard' where you and I, 'with one quick look', 'perceive three wineglasses on a table'.[7] Two or three times Funes 'reconstructed an entire day' without once erring or faltering, 'but each reconstruction had itself taken an entire day'. Having found not only that the task he set himself was interminable, but that the whole idea of such a task was pointless, Funes complained: 'My memory, sir, is like a garbage heap.' Having explored the curse and the blessings of ignorance, Milan Kundera chimes in: 'If someone could retain in his memory everything he had experienced, if he could at any time call up any fragment of his past, he would be nothing like human beings; neither his loves nor his friendships nor his angers nor his capacity to forgive or avenge would resemble ours.'[8]

And Kundera warns that we won't understand a thing about human life if we deny that at any time of that life 'a reality no longer is what it was when it was: it cannot be reconstructed.'

Hiding behind a mysterious medieval writer Suárez Miranda, Borges wrote of an empire where 'the Art of Cartography attained such Perfection that the map of a single Province occupied the entirety of a City, and the map of the Empire, the entirety of a Province. In time, those Unconscionable Maps no longer satisfied, and the Cartographers Guild struck a map of the Empire whose size was that of the Empire, and which coincided point for point with it.'[9] Pity that the latter map was found by its prospective users useless – and hence 'delivered to the Inclemencies of Sun and Winters' so that only 'Tattered Ruins of that Map, inhabited by Animals and Beggars' remained . . .

To *know* is to *choose*. In the factory of knowledge, the *product* is separated from *waste*, and it is the vision of the prospective clients, of their needs or their desires, that decides which is which. The factory of knowledge is incomplete without waste disposal sites. It is courtesy of the surrounding darkness that the light of knowledge illuminates. Knowledge is inconceivable without ignorance, memory without forgetting. Knowledge can be had thanks to laying out the blank spots of lack of interest, and the precision, exactitude, pragmatic utility of knowledge grows with the size of those spots. For all practical intents and purposes, things excluded – thrown out of focus, cast in the shadow, forced into the vague or invisible background – no longer belong to 'what is'. They have been denied existence and a room of their own in the *Lebenswelt*. They have been thereby destroyed – but this was a *creative destruction*. 'Eliminating', Mary Douglas famously said, 'is not a negative movement, but a positive effort to organize the environment.'[10]

First comes a vision: the image of the mind-boggling complexity and incapacitating infinity of the world reduced to endurable, absorbable, manageable, livable-with proportions. 'As perceivers', says Douglas, 'we select from all the stimuli falling on our senses . . . In a chaos of shifting impressions, each of us constructs a stable world in which objects have recognizable shapes.'[11]

Then comes the effort to raise the 'really existing' world (that world which is so tangibly, stubbornly, weightily and all-too-painfully present around and inside us precisely for being messy and anything but perfect) to the level of the vision; to make it as straightforward, pure, legible as the vision is. It is the vision that presents the world as amenable to moulding, kneading, squeezing and stretching – just the right object for action. As Siegried Kracauer put it, 'the weightiness, ungainliness, and impenetrability of reality are revealed clearly and more distinctly to those who approach it from the vantage point of the idea.'[12] It is thanks to the vision that the world 'emerges with horrible clarity' and the call to action is heard.

'In chasing dirt, in papering, decorating, tidying, we are not governed by anxiety to escape disease,' says Mary Douglas, 'but are positively re-ordering our environment, making it conform to an idea . . . In short, our pollution behaviour is the reaction which condemns any object or idea likely to confuse or contradict cherished classifications'[13] (or, as Calvino's Marco Polo would say, any object or idea that confounds the comforting clarity of 'the city we speak of', of the city that 'has much of what is needed to exist', what *we* need to exist – and of the way *we* speak of that city).

Left to its own devices, unlit by the spotlights of the story and before the first fitting session with the designers, the world is neither orderly nor chaotic, neither clean nor dirty. It is human design that conjures up disorder *together with* the vision of order, dirt together with the project of purity. The thought trims the image of the world first, so that the world itself can be trimmed right after. Once the image has been trimmed, the trimming of the world (the desire to trim it, the effort to trim it – though not necessarily the feat of the trimming accomplished) are a foregone conclusion. The world is manageable and demands to be managed, in as far as it has been remade to the measure of human comprehension. Francis Bacon's injunction 'Nature, to be commanded, must be obeyed' was not an intimation of humility and even less a counsel of meekness. It was an act of defiance.

Nature has been obeyed – willy-nilly, knowingly or not – since the beginning of time. Being not of human making and so stretching beyond human reach and eluding human power was, after all, the very meaning of the idea of 'Nature'. Bacon's heresy lay in the idea that nature so understood need not and should not be let alone, as owing to regrettable neglect and unforgivable lack of resolve it had heretofore been, but can be *commanded* – providing we learn its laws that need to be obeyed. Three centuries later Karl Marx would reprimand philosophers for failing to follow Bacon's precept to the end: travelling along the track leading from obedience to command, philosophers stopped halfway and left the train at the station Explanation. But, Marx would say, with all the honeycomb's perfection even the most wretched and bungling architect is superior to a bee, and that is thanks to the image of the finished product that he holds in his head before the work of construction starts.

Designs, of course, are called for because something *new* is about to be created; something extant, present already out there, in the world as it is, is to be changed. And just as the proof of the pudding is in the eating, knowledge proves itself by changing the world.

There are, though, two radically different ways of creating the new. Lewis Mumford used the allegory of farming versus mining to capture the difference between them. Agriculture, says Mumford, 'returns deliberately what man subtracts from the earth'. The process of mining, on the contrary, 'is destructive . . . and what is once taken out of the quarry or the pithead cannot be replaced'. Mining, therefore, 'presents the very image of human discontinuity, here today and gone tomorrow, now feverish with gain, now depleted and vacant'.[14] We may say that a fashion most commonly deployed among the modern ways to create (or should we rather say to creatively destroy?) has been shaped after the pattern and in the likeness of mining.

Farming stands for continuity: one grain is replaced by more grain, one sheep gives birth to more sheep. *Plus ça change – plus c'est la même chose.* The growth as reassertion and reaffirmation of being . . . A growth without losses . . . Nothing is lost on the way. Death is followed by rebirth. No wonder that societies of farmers took eternal continuity of beings for granted; what they witnessed and what they practised was an uninterrupted chain of endings indistinguishable from the incessant repetition of beginning – nay a perpetual resurrection. They did not live towards death as Martin Heidegger, pondering the ways and means of techne at the time of its ultimate triumph, suggested, but towards perpetual rebirth, whether in the form of an infinite reincarnation or of fleshy mortal bodies reborn as spirits, as immaterial but immortal souls.

Mining on the other hand is an epitome of rupture and discontinuity. The new cannot be born unless something is discarded, thrown away or destroyed. The new is created in the course of meticulous and merciless dissociation between the target product and everything else that stands in the way of its arrival. Whether precious or base, pure metals can be obtained only by removing slag and cinders from the ore. And one can get down to the ore only by removing and disposing of layer after layer of the soil that bars access to the ledge – having first cut down or burnt out the forest that barred access to the soil. Mining denies that death carries in its womb a new birth. Instead, mining proceeds on the assumption that the birth of the new requires the death of the old. And if so, then each new creation is bound to share sooner or later in the lot of that which has been left behind to rot and decompose to pave the way for a yet newer creation. Each point through which mining proceeds is a point of no return. Mining is a one-way movement, irreversible and irrevocable. The chronicle of mining is a graveyard of used up, repudiated and abandoned lodes and shafts. Mining is inconceivable without *waste*.

Asked how he obtained the beautiful harmony of his sculptures, Michelangelo reputedly answered: 'Simple. You just take a slab of marble and cut out all the superfluous bits.' In the heyday of the Renaissance, Michelangelo proclaimed the precept that was to guide modern creation. *Separation and destruction of waste was to be the trade secret of modern creation*: through cutting out and throwing away the superfluous, the needless and the useless, the beautiful, the harmonious, the pleasing and the gratifying was to be divined.

The vision of a perfect form hidden inside the formless slab of raw stone precedes its birth-act. Waste is the wrapping that conceals that form. To lay the form bare, to make it emerge and be, to admire its perfection in all its unalloyed harmony and beauty, the form must first be unwrapped. For something to be created, something else must be consigned to waste. The wrapping – the waste of the creative act – must be torn apart, shredded and disposed of lest it clutter the floor and cramp the sculptor's moves. There can be no artistic workshop without a rubbish heap.

This however makes waste into an indispensable ingredient of the creative process. More: it endows waste with an awesome, truly magic power, equivalent to that of the alchemists' philosopher's stone – the power of a wondrous transmutation of base, paltry and menial stuff into a noble, beautiful and precious object. It also makes waste an embodiment of ambivalence. Waste is simultaneously divine and satanic. It is the midwife of all creation – and its most formidable obstacle. Waste is sublime: a unique blend of attraction and repulsion arousing an equally unique mixture of awe and fear.

But remember Mary Douglas: no objects *are* 'waste' by their intrinsic qualities, and no objects can *become* waste through their inner logic. It is by being assigned to waste by human designs that material objects, whether human or inhuman, acquire all the mysterious, awe-inspiring, fearsome and repulsive qualities listed above. In his remarkable study of the ritual significance and magical proprieties commonly ascribed to human hair, Edmund Leach notes that in many cultures

> head hair, while it is a part of the body, is treated with loving care, oiled and combed and dressed in the most elaborate fashion, but as soon as it is cut off it becomes 'dirt', and is explicitly and consciously associated with the . . . polluting substances, faeces, urine, semen and sweat . . . The 'dirt' is clearly magical stuff; it endows the barber and the washerman with dangerous aggressive power, but it is not the power of a particular individual . . .

it is the power of the 'magic hair' itself, or more correctly of the remarkable act of transmutation performed through its detachment from the human body. All the operations performed on the hair – cutting, shaving or styling – amount to a conjuring up of a new person out of the old, since in many cultures head hair is remodelled as an integral part of a rite of passage from one socially allocated identity to another. And so the act of separation 'not only creates two categories of persons; it also creates a third entity, the thing that is ritually separated . . .' In other words, 'it is the ritual situation which makes the hair "powerful", not the hair which makes the ritual powerful.'[15]

The cut-off hair shares some of its imputed magical attributes (black magic, to be precise) with urine, sweat and other similarly 'polluting' substances that are shunned and abhorred because of the ambiguity of their status – trespassing on the barricade that should not be crossed lest the world lose its transparency and actions their clarity – because of the questioning and compromising of the sacrosanct boundary between the embodied self and the rest of the world. But the cut-off hair also shares in the potent and sinister attributes of all waste. Like all waste, it is instrumental in the miraculous act of extracting the new out of the old, the better out of the worse, the superior out of the inferior. That coveted and welcome transmutation is not complete, and certainly not secure, as long as the 'waste' is still around instead of having been swept away and deposited in a leak-proof, distant location. The act of creation reaches its culmination, completion and true fulfilment in the act of the separation and disposal of waste.

The modern mind was born together with the idea that *the world can be changed*. Modernity is about rejecting the world as it has been thus far and the resolution to change it. The modern way of being consists in compulsive, obsessive change: in the refutation of what 'merely is' in the name of what could, and by the same token ought, to be put in its place. The modern world is a world containing a desire, and a determination, to defy its *mêmete* (as Paul Ricoeur would say) – its sameness. A desire to make *itself* different from what the self is, to remake itself, and to go on remaking it. The modern condition is to be on the move. The choice is to modernize or perish. Modern history has therefore been a history of designing and a museum/graveyard of designs tried, used up, rejected and abandoned in the ongoing war of conquest and/or attrition waged against nature.

When it came to designing, the modern mind had no equals. Designs were one article of which modern societies, and their members, never ran short. The history of the modern era has been a long string of contemplated, attempted, pursued, seen through, failed or abandoned designs. Designs were many and different, but each one painted a future reality different from the one the designers knew. And since 'the future' does not exist as long as it remains 'in the future', and since in dealing with the non-existent one cannot 'get one's facts straight', there was no telling in advance, let alone with certainty, what the world emerging at the other end of the efforts of construction would be. Would it indeed be, as anticipated, a benign, user-friendly and pleasurable world, and would the assets budgeted and laid aside for the purpose and the approved work schedules prove adequate for transferring that world from the drawing board into the future present?

A high probability of negative answers to both questions was always and always will remain an undetachable attribute of designing. 'The idea of an unalloyed good seems to be drawn from an illusion,' warns Tzvetan Todorov.[16] Greater good can only be had at a price: alongside its benefits, it is bound to bring consequences as undesirable as they are unpredictable, though the latter are usually played down or ignored at the designing stage on the pretext of the nobility of the overall intentions. Designs are fraught with risks; as modern times went by, an ever larger part of the designing zeal and design-drawing efforts was prompted by the urge to detoxicate, neutralize or remove out of sight the 'collateral damage' done by past designing. Designing becomes its own paramount cause; designing is, ultimately, a self-perpetuating process. It is also an intrinsically wasteful endeavour. If no design can be fully and truly 'on target' and cannot but affect, in an unpredictable and often unprepossessing fashion, aspects of reality overlooked or deliberately left out of account – then only excessive designing, a *surplus of designs*, may salvage the designing process as a whole, compensating for the unavoidable fallibility of each of its parts and stages.

A foolproof, risk-proof design is very nearly a contradiction in terms.

To be seen as 'realistic', as capable of implementation, design needs to simplify the world's complexity. It must set apart the 'relevant' from the 'irrelevant', strain the manageable fragments of reality out of such parts as are resistant to manipulation, and focus on the objectives which are rendered 'reasonable' and 'within our power' by currently available means and skills, supplemented by means and skills it is hoped will be acquired soon.

Between them, all the conditions listed, in order to be met, require that a lot of things be cast aside – out of view, out of thought and out of action. They also require that whatever has been left out is turned – turns immediately – into the *waste* of the designing process. The underlying strategy and the inevitable effect of designing is the division of the material outcomes of the action into 'what counts' and 'what does not count', into the 'useful product' and 'waste'. Because the drawing of designs is (for the reasons spelled out before) bound not only to be continuous but also to continuously expand in volume, designing cannot but portend a perpetual accumulation of waste and an unstoppable growth of unresolved or perhaps unresolvable waste disposal problems.

On 29 November 2002, I set four 'search engines' to find the websites referring to the notion of 'waste'. Altavista returned 6,353,800 website addresses. Google found 11,500,000 (with a proviso: 'around'; Google prides itself on the speed of its web-scanning and this one took a bare 0.07 seconds). Lycos found 17,457,433 websites. Alltheweb found 17,478,410.

Let me observe on this occasion that an unsolicited bonus effect of my search for information about 'waste' was, as you can see from those figures, the oblique information on its *excess*: of that loyal, till-death-us-do-part ally and accomplice of waste and the principal contributor to its colossal and exponentially swelling obesity. By no stretch of imagination could the volume of infor-mation 'available' and 'on offer' be even perfunctorily perused, let alone absorbed, digested and retained. In our present-day strategy of fighting risks with the weapon of excess, waste is preprogrammed, and the rise and rise of information is an excel-lent example of the universal trend. The excess of information is too much to be dumped into human brains – or even into its conventional repository, the library shelves. The invention of the electronic memory came in handy: the world wide web fills the bill of an infinitely capacious, and exponentially growing, waste-information disposal bin. The universal wastefulness characteristic of all modern production has found its possibly most spectacular manifestation in the insatiable thirst of information, which has been laid bare thanks to computer technology. 'Information is principally endless in cyberspace and this creates an abstract need for control of information that can never in fact be satisfied . . . What can be called the technopower spiral is constituted out of three elements: information overload, mastering overload with a tool, and the occurrence of information overload,' writes Tim Jordan. We may say that the production of informational waste, like all waste-producing activity, is self-propelling: efforts of waste disposal turn out more waste. 'Problems of information overload tend to re-emerge with the devices that become essential to information management themselves producing too much information.'[17]

But let me return to the results of my search.

Even by the standards of our world, known to be thrown repeatedly into disarray by the no longer absorbable and so unmanageable excess of 'objectively available' information, rather than by its shortage, the number of entries dealing with the issue of waste is enormous. Just how enormous can be gathered if comparison is made with other issues yet more salient and conspicuous on the public agenda and more explicitly debated, issues currently on everybody's tongue and ostensibly on everybody's mind. The Alltheweb search engine returned on the same day 7,304,625 websites for terrorism, currently the hottest talk of the global telecity, 6,547,193 sites for poverty, 3,727,070 for unemployment, 3,017,330 for racism and 1,508,426 for famine. One may guess that the issue of waste, though hitting the front-page headlines relatively seldom, has earned a steady and permanent place among contemporary concerns worldwide. Given that the comparative rarity of its appearances in the speeches of public figures and in manifestos and party platforms hardly matches the extent of the subterranean concerns as evidenced by the record-breaking number of concerned websites, waste may be described as *simultaneously a most harrowing problem and a most closely guarded secret* of our times. 'Waste', we may say, taking hint from Calvino, belongs to the Aglaura that 'grows on the ground' but not to the Aglaura the Aglaurians 'grow with' . . .

The story we grow in and with has no interest in waste. According to that story it is the product that matters, not the waste. Two kinds of trucks leave factory yards daily – one kind of truck proceeds to the warehouses and department stores, the other to the rubbish tips. The story we have grown with has trained us to note (count, value, care for) solely the first kind of truck. Of the second, we think only on the (fortunately not-yet-daily) occasions when the avalanche of leftovers descends from the refuse mountains and breaks through the fences meant to protect our own backyards. We do not visit those mountains, neither in body nor in thought, as we do not stroll through rough districts, mean streets, urban ghettoes, asylum-seekers' camps and other no-go areas. We carefully avoid them (or are directed away from them) in our compulsive tourist escapades. We dispose of leftovers in the most radical and effective way: we make them invisible by not looking and unthinkable by not thinking. They worry us only when the routine elementary defences are broken and the precautions fail – when the comfortable, soporific insularity of our *Lebenswelt* which they were supposed to protect is in danger.

But if you asked Lycos or Alltheweb, each would offer you more than 17 million testimonies that such a moment of worry is just round the corner. It may come any time now. Perhaps it has already arrived.

Waste is the dark, shameful secret of all production. Preferably, it would remain a secret. Captains of industry would rather not mention it at all – they need to be pressed hard to admit it. And yet the strategy of excess, unavoidable in a life lived-towards-a-design, the strategy that prods, invigorates and whips up productive effort and so also the output of waste, makes the cover-up a tall order. The sheer mass of waste would not allow it to be glossed over and silenced out of existence. Hence the waste-disposal industry is one branch of modern production (alongside the security service, that continuation of the cover-up policy by other means, aimed at staving off the return of the repressed – of which more later) that will never work itself out of its job. Modern survival – the survival of the modern form of life – depends on the dexterity and proficiency of garbage removal.

Rubbish collectors are the unsung heroes of modernity. Day in day out, they refresh and make salient again the borderline between normality and pathology, health and illness, the desirable and the repulsive, the accepted and the rejected, the *comme il faut* and *comme il ne faut pas*, the inside and the outside of the human universe. That borderline needs their constant vigilance and diligence because it is anything but a 'natural frontier': no sky-high mountain ranges, bottomless seas or impassable gorges separate the inside from the outside. And it is not the difference between useful products and waste that begs and plies the boundary. Quite the contrary, it is the boundary that divines, literally conjures up, the difference between them – the difference between the admitted and the rejected, the included and the excluded.

That boundary is drawn afresh with every round of garbage collection and removal. Its sole existential mode is the incessant *activity* of separation. No wonder that it cannot be left unattended; it requires constant servicing, lest the border posts and control booths disintegrate and indescribable turmoil follows. No wonder that the boundary oozes anxiety and strains the nerves. All boundaries beget ambivalence, but this one is exceptionally fertile. However hard one tries, the frontier separating the 'useful product' from 'waste' is a grey zone: a kingdom of underdefinition, uncertainty – and danger.

Too much depends on the proper servicing of the boundary to leave the task to the discretion of the dustmen alone. Rubbish collectors may err, be absent-minded, lazy or sloppy. Their eccentric judgements may bring back the very ambivalence that the strict and legible borderline was meant to eliminate. Since the boundary precedes the division between the intended products and all remainders consigned to the refuse category, drawing the borderline in a no-room-for-mistake manner and keeping it tight and impermeable needs a lot of expertise and skill – but even more it needs an authority which may hopefully compensate for the dearth of both. Immigration officers and quality controllers are needed. They are to stand guard on the line separating order from chaos (a battle line or armistice line, but always suspected of inviting trespassers and being ready for conflagration). They are the elite units of the frontline troops in the modern war against ambivalence.

Designing 'makes sense' in as far as not everything in the extant world is as it *should* be. More importantly yet, it comes into its own if that world is not what it *could* be, considering the available or hoped-for means of making things different. The aim of designing is to plot more room for 'the good' and less room, or no room, for 'the bad'. It is the good that makes the bad what it is: bad. 'The bad' is the waste of improvement.

Granted, nature is ruled by its laws. Laws of nature have not been made by humans, and so cannot be unmade by humans. Following Bacon's advice, humans could only learn those laws so that they could use them to human advantage. One aspect of the world which the modern mind found particularly unsavoury, unacceptable and unbearable was, however, the state of humanity; and humanity was one part of the world that managed to ignore, to its own peril, the laws of nature, and to replace them by man-made laws.

Guided by man-made laws, humanity plodded on while buffeted, tousled, hurt and grieved by forces of unreason, prejudice and superstition. Compared with the inhuman part of the universe that knows not of 'mistake', the human past could only appear as a greenhouse of stupidity and ill-will, and a long sequence of blunders and crimes. The sole 'law of human history' one could think of was the necessity for reason to take over where human spontaneity spectacularly failed. The takeover was as unavoidable as it was urgent. The takeover was a historical inevitability. It was bound to happen, thanks to the sheer absence of choice; to the indispensability of the discovery that at some point human reason must take charge of history, stamp out, tame or muzzle its natural inclinations and elemental tendencies, and assume responsibility for the shape of historical necessity.

Such a point seemed to have been reached at the threshold of the modern era, when the old pattern of human togetherness could no longer hold and society appeared to fall apart at its seams. Continuation of the status quo, dubbed *ancient regime*, would be an abomination: a violation of the law of history and a criminal offence against human reason. Replacement of the flawed legacy of licentious, unaccountable and unruly history with new, designed from scratch, reason dictated, made-to-order and monitored (refined, civilized, *policés*) patterns of human togetherness could no longer be delayed. That imperative was to become the prime mover of modernizing zeal.

Modernity, we may say, is a state of perpetual emergency – inspired and fed, to quote Geoffrey Bennington writing in another context, by 'a sense that someone has to give orders if all is not to be lost'.[18] Without us – a deluge. Without preventive actions or pre-empting strikes – a catastrophe. The alternative to a pre-designed future is the rule of chaos. Things human cannot be left to their own course.

Modernity is a condition of compulsive, and addictive, designing.

Where is design, there is waste. No house is really finished before the building site has been swept clean of unwanted leftovers.

When it comes to designing the forms of human togetherness, the waste is human beings. Some human beings who do not fit into the designed form nor can be fitted into it. Or such as adulterate its purity and so becloud its transparency: Kafka's monsters and mutants, like the nondescript Odradek or the crossbred of kitten and lamb – oddities, miscreants, hybrids who call the bluff of ostensibly inclusive/exclusive categories. Blots on the otherwise elegant and serene landscape. Flawed beings, from whose absence or obliteration the designed form could only gain, becoming more uniform, more harmonious, more secure and altogether more at peace with itself.

Another name for the designation of the new and improved forms of human togetherness is order-building. Order: according to the *Oxford English Dictionary*, 'the condition in which everything is in its proper place, and performs its proper function'. To order (to build order where chaos ruled): 'to set or keep in order or proper condition; to dispose according to rule; to regulate, govern, manage'.

The prospect of order (any new prospect of any new order) draws out from its lair the ogre of chaos. Chaos is the order's alter ego, an order with a negative sign: a condition in which something *is not* in its proper place and *does not* perform its proper function (if, that is, a place and a function proper for it are at all conceivable). That 'something' with no abode and no function strides the barricade separating order from chaos. Its excision is the last act of creation before the completion of order-building labours.

There could be no order without chaos, just as there would be no heads without tails and no light without darkness. Chaos reveals itself as a state of chaos by allowing events that the order must already have prohibited; but the moment the prohibition was announced, chaos would have bared its face without delay. Chaos, disorder, lawlessness portends the infinity of possibilities and the limitlessness of inclusion; order stands for limits and finitude. In an orderly (ordered) space, not *everything* may happen.

Orderly space is a rule-governed space, whereas the rule is a rule in as far as it forbids and excludes. Law becomes a law once it exempts from the realm of the permitted acts that would be allowed to be done were it not for the presence of law – and actors who would be allowed to dwell in the state of lawlessness. Law, as Giorgio Agamben put it,

> is made of nothing but what it manages to capture inside itself through the inclusive exclusion of the *exceptio*: it nourishes itself on this exception and is a dead letter without it . . . Exception does not subtract itself from the rule; rather, the rule, suspending itself, gives rise to the exception and, maintaining itself in relation to the exception, first constitutes itself as a rule.[19]

All initiative stays steadfastly on the side of the rule. *The rule precedes reality.* Legislation precedes the ontology of the human world. The law is a design, a blueprint for a clearly circumscribed, legibly marked, mapped and signposted habitat. It is the law that brings lawlessness into being by drawing the line dividing the inside from the outside. Lawlessness is not a mere absence of law; lawlessness arises with the withdrawal, suspension, refusal of law. The law's bid to universality would sound hollow were it not for the law's inclusion of the exempted through its own withdrawal. Law would never reach universality without its right to draw the

limit to its application, creating by the same token a universal category of the exempted/excluded, and the right to lay out an 'out
of bounds', providing thereby the dumping ground for the ones
who are excluded, recycled into human waste.

Looked at from the viewpoint of law, exemption is the act of
self-suspension. Self-suspension means that the law confines its
concern with the exempted/excluded to holding them outside the
rule-governed realm which it has circumscribed. Law acts on that
concern by proclaiming the exempted to be not its concern. There
is no law for the excluded. The condition of being excluded consists in the absence of law that applies to it.

In Agamben's characterization, the ideal-typical model of an
excluded being is offered by the *homo sacer*, a category of ancient
Roman law 'set outside human jurisdiction without being brought
into the realm of divine law'.[20] The life of a *homo sacer* is devoid
of value, whether in the human or in the divine perspective.
Killing a *homo sacer* is not a punishable offence, but neither can
the life of a *homo sacer* be used in a religious sacrifice. Stripped of
human and divine significance that only law can bestow, the life
of a *homo sacer* is worthless. Killing a *homo sacer* is neither crime
nor sacrilege, but for the same reason it cannot be an offering.

Translating all that into contemporary secular terms we would
say that in its present-day version the *homo sacer* is neither defined
by any set of positive laws nor a carrier of human rights that
precede legal rules. It is by the sovereign's capacity to refuse the
grant of positive laws and to deny the possession of any rights of
alternative origin (including 'human rights'), and therefore by its
capacity to set aside the *homini sacri* defined by the withdrawal
of legal definitions, that the 'sovereign sphere' is claimed, gained,
circumscribed and protected. 'The political sphere of sovereignty
was . . . constituted through a double exclusion.'[21]

Homo sacer is the principal category of human waste laid out in
the course of the modern production of orderly (law abiding, rule
governed) sovereign realms. To quote Agamben one further time:

> All well-meaning chatter notwithstanding, the idea of a people
> today is nothing other than the empty support of state identity and

is recognized as such. For those who might still nurture some doubt on the matter, it would be instructive to take a look at what is happening around us from this point of view: on the one hand, the world powers take up arms to defend a *state without a people* (Kuwait), and, on the other hand, the *people without a state* (Kurds, Armenians, Palestinians, Basques, Jews of the Diaspora) can be oppressed and exterminated with impunity, so as to make clear that the destiny of a people can only be a state identity and that the concept of *people* makes sense only if recodified within the concept of citizenship.[22]

Throughout the era of modernity, the nation-state has claimed the right to preside over the distinction between order and chaos, law and lawlessness, citizen and *homo sacer,* belonging and exclusion, useful (= legitimate) product and waste. 'All well-meaning chatter notwithstanding', sifting out, segregating and disposing of the waste of order-building combined into the main preoccupation and metafunction of the state, as well as providing the foundation for its claims to authority.

The exclusive and undivided monopoly of the state over the performance of that function went uncontested – not contested by other states at any rate, eager as they must have been to sustain the aura of naturalness and unexceptionality around a settlement specific to the era of reshaping human realities in the likenesses of designs. For most practical purposes, that monopoly remains uncontested even today, despite the accumulating evidence of the fictional status of the state's claims to sovereignty. In order to salvage whatever is left of state sovereignty in its present-day phantom-like incarnation, the orthodox ways and means, complete with their customary legitimations, are routinely resorted to.

Present-day nation-states may no longer preside over the drawing of blueprints and exercise the ownership right of *utere et abutere* (use and misuse) over the sites of order-building, but they still claim the foundational, constitutive prerogative of sovereignty: their right of exemption.

2

Are there too many of them?

Or the waste of economic progress

There are always too many of *them*. 'Them' are the fellows of whom there should be fewer – or better still none at all. And there are never enough of us. 'Us' are the folks of whom there should be more.

On the authority of the *Oxford English Dictionary*, no use of the word 'overpopulation' had been recorded until the late nineteenth century – 1870 to be exact. And that despite the fact that just before that century started (in 1798 to be precise) Thomas Robert Malthus published his *Essay on the Principle of Population as it Affects the Future Improvement of Society* – the book which stated bluntly that the growth of population would forever outrun the growth of food supply and that unless human fecundity is constrained there won't be enough food for everyone.

Refuting Malthus's proposition and devastating his argument was a favourite pastime of the most eminent spokespeople for the up-and-coming, boisterous and self-confident modern spirit. Indeed, Malthus's 'principle of population' went against the grain of everything the modern promise stood for – its certainty that every human misery is curable, that in the course of time solutions will be found and applied and all heretofore unsatisfied human needs met, and that science and its practical technological arm is bound sooner or later to lift human realities to the level of human potential and so put paid once and for all to the irritating gap between the 'is' and the 'ought'. That century believed (and was daily reinforced in its beliefs by the well-attuned chorus of philosophers and statesmen) that more human happiness may and will be achieved by more human power (primarily industrial and military power), and that the might and the wealth of nations are measured by the numbers of their workers and soldiers. Indeed, nothing in the part of the world where Malthus's prophecy was conceived and contested suggested that more people would lead to fewer of the goods needed for human survival. On the contrary, labour power and fighting power, the larger the better, seemed to be the principal and the most effective cure for the bane of scarcity. There were infinitely vast and fabulously rich lands around the globe spattered with blank spots and barely populated, virtually empty territories waiting for conquest and colonization; but huge, fully manned industrial plants and formidable armies were needed to invade and hold them. Big was beautiful – and profitable. Big populations meant big power. Big power meant big land acquisitions. Big land acquisitions meant big wealth. Big lands and big wealth meant room for a big number of people. QED.

And so if a thought that there are too many people around to be fed did occur to people concerned with the state of affairs inside their countries, the answer seemed to them obvious, convincing and credible, even if paradoxical: a therapy for the excess of population is more population. Only the most vigorous, and so most populous nations will develop the muscle needed to overwhelm and subdue or push aside the wan, backward and irresolute or decadent and degenerating occupants of the globe, and only such nations will be able to flex that muscle to great effect. If the word 'overpopulation' was at that time on offer, it would be treated as an oxymoron. There cannot be 'too many of *us*' – it is the opposite, being too few, that should be a reason to worry. Local congestion can be globally unloaded. Local problems will be globally resolved.

Expressing what had by then become virtually the common view of the country, one of the speakers at the Trades Union Congress convened in 1883 (a Mr Toyne from Saltburn) noted with grave concern

> a tendency in the rural districts to monopolize the land; to convert small farms into large ones. The small farmsteads were being

knocked down, and the land absorbed into large estates. The present land system was driving men off the land into the mines and factories to compete against the artisan in the labour market. The working men of the country wanted relief from this immediately.[1]

The complaint was by no means new – only the suspected culprits and prospective defendants were different in a diagnosis repeated monotonously throughout the turbulent history of creative destruction known under the name of economic progress. This time, the overcrowding of the labour market was blamed on the ruin and downfall of smallholders prompted by new agricultural technology. A few decades before, the disintegration of artisan guilds triggered by industrial machinery was pointed to as the prime cause of misery. A few decades later the turn was to come of the mines and factories in which the victims of agricultural progress once sought salvation. And yet in all such cases the way to release the pressure on the life conditions of labourers and to improve their living standards was sought in a thinning out of the crowds besieging the gates of the establishment offering employment. That solution seemed obvious and caused no controversy as there was no shortage of places on to which the surplus could be expeditiously unloaded. As Joseph Arch, the legendary leader of the Agricultural Workers' Union, testified in 1881 before Her Majesty's Commissioners of Agriculture:

Q. How do you set about ensuring the labourers' getting higher wages?

A. We have reduced the number of labourers in the market very considerably.

Q. How have you reduced the number of labourers in the market?

A. We have emigrated about 700,000 souls, men, women and children, within the last eight or nine years.

Q. How have these 700,000 souls been emigrated; out of which funds?

A. I went over to Canada, and I made arrangements with the Canadian Government to give them so much and we found so much from the funds of the trade.[2]

Another factor prompting the export of internally produced 'social problems' through a massive deportation of the affected part of the population was the fear that the accumulation of the 'redundant' inside the cities would reach a critical point of self-combustion. Sporadic yet repeated outbursts of urban unrest spurred the powers-that-be into action. After June 1848 the 'rough districts' of Paris were cleansed wholesale of rebellious *misérables* and the 'great unwashed' were transported *en masse* overseas, to Algeria. After the Paris Commune of 1871 the exercise was repeated, though this time New Caledonia was selected as the destination.[3]

From the very beginning, the modern era was a time of great migration. Uncounted so far and perhaps uncountable masses of population moved around the globe, leaving their native countries which offered no livelihood for foreign lands that promised a better fortune. The popular and prevalent trajectories changed over time, depending on the drifts of the current 'hot spots' of modernization, but on the whole the migrants wandered from 'more developed' (more intensely modernizing) parts of the planet to the 'undeveloped' (not yet thrown out of socioeconomic balance under the impact of modernization) areas.

The itineraries were, so to speak, overdetermined. On the one hand, surplus population unable to find gainful employment or maintain its previously earned or inherited social status in its country of origin was a phenomenon confined by and large to the terrains of advanced modernizing processes. On the other, thanks to the same factor of rapid modernization, the countries in which the surplus population was produced enjoyed (even if temporarily) a technological and military superiority over the territories yet untouched by modernizing processes. This allowed them to view and treat such areas as 'void' (and to make them void in the event that the natives resisted being pushed, or wielded a nuisance power which the settlers found too irksome for comfort) and thus as ready, and clamouring, for massive settlement. By estimates that are obviously incomplete, about 30–50 million natives of 'pre-modern' lands, about 80 per cent of their total population, were wiped out between the time of the first arrival and settlement of

European soldiers and traders and the beginning of the twentieth century, when their numbers reached their lowest point.[4] Many were murdered, many others perished of imported diseases, and the rest died out after losing the ways that for centuries kept their ancestors alive. As Charles Darwin summed up the saga of the Europe-led process of 'civilizing the savages': 'Where the European has trod, death seems to pursue the aboriginal.'[5]

Ironically, the extermination of aborigines for the sake of clearing new sites for Europe's surplus population (that is, priming the sites for the role of dumping ground for the human waste which economic progress at home was turning out in growing quantities) was carried in the name of the self-same progress that recycled the surplus of Europeans into 'economic migrants'. And so, for instance, Theodore Roosevelt represented the extermination of American Indians as a selfless service to the cause of civilization: 'The settler and pioneer have at bottom had justice on their side: this great continent could not have been kept as nothing but a game preserve for squalid savages.'[6] While General Roca, the commander of the infamous episode in Argentinian history euphemistically dubbed 'Conquest of the Desert' but consisting of the 'ethnic cleansing' of the pampas of its Indian population, explained to his fellow countrymen that their self-respect obliged them 'to put down as soon as possible, by reason or by force, this handful of savages who destroy our wealth and prevent us from definitely occupying, in the name of law, progress and our own security, the richest and most fertile lands of the Republic'.[7]

Many years have passed since then, but the viewpoints, the sights they open up and the words used to describe the sights have not changed. Quite recently the Israeli government decided to cleanse the Negev desert of its Bedouin population to make way for settlements of the next wave of Jewish immigrants.[8] Already five years before, as if anticipating the future need for empty lands into which to unload the overcrowded northern towns, Ariel Sharon (Interior Minister at the time) declared the Bedouin already gone. The Negev, he said, was empty 'but for a few goats and sheep'. The later action brought reality closer to Sharon's verdict: of 140,000 Negev Bedouin, about half have thus far been settled in 'recognized villages' or 'development towns' 'that are little better than sprawling urban dumps'. Speaking on behalf of the Jewish Agency, its treasurer Shai Hermesh opined that 'the trouble with the Bedouin is they're still on the edge between tradition and civilization . . . They say their mothers and grandmothers want to live with the sheep around them.' But his conclusion was optimistic for civilization's prospects: we need the Negev, he said, for the next generation of Jewish immigrants. In the Negev 'you can get land for pennies.'

'Overpopulation' is a fiction of actuaries: a code name for the appearance of a number of people who, instead of helping the smooth functioning of economy, make the attainment, let alone the rise, of indices by which the proper functioning is measured and evaluated all that much more difficult. The numbers of such people seem to grow uncontrollably, continually adding to expenses yet nothing to gains. In a society of producers, they are the people whose labour cannot be usefully deployed since all the goods that the existing and prospective demand is able to absorb may be produced, and produced more swiftly, profitably and 'economically', without keeping them in jobs. In a society of consumers, they are 'flawed consumers' – people lacking the money that would allow them to stretch the capacity of the consumer market, while they create another kind of demand to which the profit-oriented consumer industry cannot respond and which it cannot profitably 'colonize'. Consumers are the prime assets of consumer society; flawed consumers are its most irksome and costly liabilities.

'Surplus population' is one more variety of human waste. Unlike *homini sacri*, the 'lives unworthy of living', the victims of order-building designs, they are not 'legitimate targets' exempted from the protection of law at the sovereign's behest. They are rather unintended and unplanned 'collateral casualties' of economic progress. In the course of economic progress (the principal assembly/disassembly line of modernization) the extant forms of 'making a living' are successively dismantled, broken up into components meant to be reassembled ('recycled') into new forms. In the process some components are damaged beyond repair, while of those that survive the dismantling phase only a reduced quantity is needed to compose the new, as a rule smarter and slimmer, working contraptions.

Unlike in the case of the legitimate targets of order-building, no one plans collateral casualties of economic progress, let alone draws in advance the line separating the damned from the saved. No one gives the commands, no one bears the responsibility, as the baffled and desperate hero of John Steinbeck's *Grapes of Wrath* learned much to his dismay: wishing to fight, gun in hand, in defence of his no longer 'economically viable' farm, he could not find a single malevolent perpetrator of his torment and distress to shoot. Being but a sideline of economic progress, the production of human waste has all the markings of an impersonal, purely technical issue. The principal actors in the drama are 'terms of trade', 'market demands', 'competitive pressures', 'productivity' or 'efficiency' requirements, all covering up or explicitly denying any connection with the intentions, will, decisions and actions of real humans with names and addresses.

Causes of exclusion may be different, but for those on the receiving end the results feel much the same. Faced with the daunting task of gaining the means of biological survival while stripped of the self-confidence and self-esteem needed to sustain their social survival, they have no reason to contemplate and savour the subtle distinctions between suffering by design and misery by default. They may well be excused for feeling rejected, being incensed and indignant, breathing vengeance and harbouring revenge – though having learned the futility of resistance and surrendered to the verdict of their own inferiority they could hardly find a way to recast all such sentiments into effective action. Whether by an explicit sentence or by an implied though never officially published verdict, they have become superfluous, unnecessary, unneeded and unwanted, and their reactions, off the mark or absent, render the censure a self-fulfilling prophecy.

In a brilliant insight into the condition and conduct of 'supernumerary' or 'marginalized' people, the great Polish scholar Stefan Czarnowski describes them as '*déclassés* individuals, possessing no defined social status, deemed redundant from the point of view of material and intellectual production and regarding themselves as such'. 'Organized society' treats them as 'scroungers and intruders, charges them at best with unwarranted pretences or indolence, often with all sorts of wickedness, like scheming, swindling, living a life hovering on the brink of criminality, but in each case with feeding parasitically on the social body'.[9]

Superfluous people are in a no-win situation. If they attempt to fall in line with currently lauded ways of life, they are immediately accused of sinful arrogance, false pretences and the cheek of claiming unearned bonuses – if not of criminal intent. If they openly resent and refuse to honour those ways which may be savoured by the haves but are more like poison for themselves, the have-nots, this is promptly taken as proof of what 'public opinion' (more correctly, its elected or self-appointed spokespersons) 'told you all along' – that the superfluous are not just an alien body, but a cancerous growth gnawing at the healthy tissues of society and sworn enemies of 'our way of life' and 'what we stand for'.

A hundred and thirty years after the word appeared in the English language (on 22 January 2003, to be precise) Altavista returned 70,384 websites dealing with 'overpopulation', Google 'around 118,000' (it took it 0.15 seconds to locate them), Lycos 336,678 and Alltheweb 337,134. These numbers do not appear to be particularly large, especially when compared with the millions of websites preoccupied with waste. But then, technically speaking, overpopulation is but one side-effect of the emergent global civilization bent on the production and disposal of waste.

'The production of superfluous bodies, which are no longer required for work, is a direct consequence of globalization,' suggests Hauke Brunkhorst. He adds that the peculiarity of the globalized version of 'overpopulation' is the way it tops off fast rising inequality with the exclusion of 'superfluous bodies' from the realm of social communication. 'For those who fall outside the functional system, be it in India, Brazil or Africa, or even at present in many districts of New York or Paris, all others soon become inaccessible. Their voice will no longer be heard, often they are literally struck dumb.'[10]

Demographers tend to cut the set of considered and estimated variables too narrowly to work out reliable forecasts of future population numbers. Based by necessity on the latest trends in birth and mortality rates, themselves given to change without notice, demographic forecasts reflect current states of mind rather than the shape of the future. They come closer to the status of prophecies than the standards usually imputed to, and expected, from scientific prediction. Demographers, to be sure, are only partly to blame for the uncertain status of the forecasts: however diligently the available data are collected and however cautiously evaluated, the fact remains that 'future history' does not present itself to a scientific study and defies even the most advanced methodology of scientific prediction. In the present state of the planet notorious for the absence of firmly institutionalized routines, demography cannot on its own take full account of the sociocultural transformations *in statu nascendi* whose direction and import are still far from being fully revealed. In particular, we can hardly visualize in advance the social settings that may define 'redundancy' and shape the human-waste disposal mechanisms of the future. It is with this proviso that the demographic estimates that follow ought to be read. They need to be interpreted primarily as evidence of present-day concerns and worries, likely soon to be disavowed, abandoned or forgotten, and replaced by other preoccupations.

According to the Earth Policy Institute report of 5 September 2002, the world population that presently numbers 6.2 billion people is rising by roughly 77 million each year, yet the growth is distributed highly unevenly. Fertility rates in the so-called 'developed countries' (that is, the block of the affluent countries of the West and the niches of fast 'Westernization' scattered elsewhere) have already fallen below the magic ratio of 2.1 children per woman, considered to be 'replacement level' (population zero growth). But the 'developing' countries, with their 5 billion people at the moment, are currently expected to reach 8.2 billion inhabitants by 2050. As the poorest countries, like Afghanistan or Angola, grow fastest, their population is expected to rise to 1.8 billion from the current 660 million.

To see past the purely numerical calculations of the impending troubles of 'overpopulation' and through to the sociocultural realities they hide rather than reveal, we need first to note that the places where the 'population bomb' is expected to explode are in most cases the parts of the planet where the population is currently the least dense. Africa, for instance, has 55 inhabitants per square mile, while there are on average 261 people per square mile living in the whole of Europe, even when the steppes and the permafrosts of Russia are included, 857 per square mile living in Japan, 1,100 in the Netherlands, 1,604 in Taiwan and 14,218 in Hong Kong. As recently pointed out by the deputy chief editor of *Forbes* magazine, if the whole population of China and India moved to continental USA, the resulting population density wouldn't exceed that of England, Holland or Belgium. And yet few people consider Holland an 'overpopulated' country, while no end of alarms are heard about the overpopulation of Africa or of the whole of Asia apart from the few 'Pacific Tigers'.

To explain the paradox, the analysts of population trends point out that there is little connection between density of settlement and the phenomenon of overpopulation: the degree of overpopulation ought to be measured in reference to the number of people to be sustained by the resources a given country owns and the capacity of the local environment to sustain human life. But, as Paul and Ann Ehrlich point out, the Netherlands can support its record-breaking density of population precisely because so many other lands cannot... In 1984–6, for instance, Holland imported about 4 million tons of cereals, 130,000 tons of oils and 480,000 tons of peas, beans and lentils, all valued relatively cheaply on the global commodity exchanges, which enabled it to produce commodities for export itself, like milk or edible meat, which attracted notoriously high prices. Rich nations can afford a high density of population because they are 'high entropy' centres, drawing resources, most notably the sources of energy, from the rest of the world, and returning in exchange the polluting, often toxic waste of industrial processing that uses up, annihilates and destroys a large part of the worldwide supplies of energy. The relatively small (by planetary standards) population of affluent countries accounts for about two-thirds of the total energy use. In a lecture with a telling title, 'Too many rich people', delivered at the International Conference on Population and Development

held in Cairo on 5–13 September 1994, Paul Ehrlich summed up
the conclusion of his and Ann Ehrlich's study:

> The impact of humanity on Earth's life support system is not just
> determined by the number of people alive on the planet. It also
> depends on how those people behave. When this is considered, an
> entirely different picture emerges: the main population problem is
> in wealthy countries. There are, in fact, too many rich people.

The Ehrlichs ask an awkward question indeed, one that literally turns upside down the picture we hold dear for the comfort
it brings and its power of absolution for the sins we know and the
sins we would rather not know about. Are we not the ones, the
rich, the carefree consumers of the planet's resources, who are
the true planetary 'parasites', 'scroungers' and 'spongers'? Is it not
so that the 'surplus' or 'excessive' fertility we blame for the 'overpopulation' of the globe needs to be traced back to 'our glorious
way of life' which our political spokespeople declare to be 'not a
matter for negotiation' and swear to defend tooth and nail?

For reasons that hardly need to be spelled out, this is a conclusion hard to accept. It seems to be in the nature of our 'overpopulation' worries, at least in their present-day version, to be
focused on 'them' not 'us'. This habit holds no mystery. After all,
the grand design that sets the 'waste' apart from the 'useful
product' does not signal an 'objective state of affairs', but the preferences of the designers. Measured by the standards of that design
(and there are no other authoritative standards) it is 'their' fertility that is wasteful, since it puts excessive, unbearable pressure on
their local 'life support system', which should rather be mined of
energy and other resources to support *our* way of life, ever more
whimsical, voracious and thirsty for fuel. It is therefore 'they' who
overpopulate our planet.

No wonder that the Earth Policy Institute, like so many other
learned institutions which the affluent world founds and funds for
our protection, has little doubt that limiting 'their' fertility is the
key to the resolution of the planet-wide 'overpopulation'
quandary. So formulated the task calls in its turn for a quick fix,
all the simpler and more straightforward for being aimed at

'them'. What is needed is technology, which we, with our omnipotent science and industry, can supply and would be happy to supply (if the price is right). And so we learn from the Institute that 'the availability of effective contraception is key' – though boosting the sorely sluggish consumer market (in other words, the production of the prospective consumers of contraceptives, nicknamed euphemistically 'increasing the level of female education and employment') is a vital condition of that commodity being sought, bought and paid for.

It was for that purpose that the Cairo conference already mentioned resolved to launch a twenty-year 'population and health programme', with 'them', the 'developing' countries, paying two-thirds of the costs and the rest paid by the 'donor' (sic!) countries. Unfortunately, though 'they' 'largely honoured their commitment', we, the 'donors', failed to honour ours and limited our part in the meant-to-be-joint operation to shipping in the pharmaceutical goods. It was because of such dilatoriness, in the opinion of the Earth Policy Institute, that 122 million women became pregnant between 1994 and 2000 . . . As it happened, an unexpected ally joined the battle against 'their' rampant fertility: AIDS. In Botswana, for instance, life expectancy dropped in the same period from 70 to 36 years, pulling the population prognosis for 2015 down by 28 per cent. Was it solely because of their greed and self-assumed guardianship of 'intellectual property rights' that our pharmaceutical companies did not show much zeal in supplying affordable weapons to fight the epidemics?

It is always the excess of *them* that worries *us*. Closer to home, it is rather the free fall of fertility rates and its inevitable consequence, the ageing of the population, that makes us fret and fume. Will there be enough of 'us' to sustain 'our way of life'? Will there be enough dustmen, collectors of the garbage which 'our way of life' daily spawns, or – as Richard Rorty asks – a sufficient number of 'people who get their hands dirty cleaning our toilets' while being paid ten times less than we 'who sit behind desks and punch keyboards'?[11] This other, unprepossessing side of the war against 'overpopulation' – the grim prospect of the need to import more rather than fewer of 'them' just to keep 'our way of life' afloat – haunts the lands of the affluent.

That prospect would not be so frightening – as it tends to be felt everywhere except in the high-security company boardrooms and tedium-oozing academic conference halls – were it not for a new use to which wasted humans, and particularly the wasted humans who have managed to land on affluent shores, have been put.

Excursus: *On the nature of human powers* Unravelling the mystery of earthly, human power Mikhail Bakhtin, one of the greatest Russian philosophers of the past century, began from the description of 'cosmic fear' – the human, all-too-human emotion aroused by the unearthly, inhuman magnificence of the universe; the kind of fear that precedes man-made power and serves it as foundation, prototype and inspiration. *Cosmic* fear is, in Bakhtin's words, the trepidation felt

> In the face of the immeasurably great and immeasurably powerful: in the face of the starry heavens, the material mass of the mountains, the sea, and the fear of cosmic upheavals and elemental disasters . . . The cosmic fear [is] fundamentally not mystical in the strict sense (being a fear in the face of the materially great and the materially indefinable power) . . .[12]

At the core of 'cosmic fear' lies, let us note, the nonentity of the frightened, wan and mortal being compared to the enormity of the everlasting universe; the sheer weakness, incapacity to resist, *vulnerability* of the frail and soft human body that the sight of the 'starry heavens' or 'the material mass of the mountains' reveals; but also the realization that it is not in human power to grasp, comprehend, mentally assimilate that awesome might which manifests itself in the sheer grandiosity of the universe. That universe escapes all understanding. Its intentions are unknown, its next steps are unpredictable. If there is a preconceived plan or logic in its action, it certainly escapes the human ability to comprehend. And so 'cosmic fear' is also the horror of the unknown: the terror of *uncertainty*.

Vulnerability and uncertainty are the two qualities of the human condition out of which 'official fear' is moulded: fear of *human* power, of man-made and man-held power. Such 'official fear' is construed after the pattern of the inhuman power reflected by (or, rather, emanating from) 'cosmic fear'.

Bakhtin suggests that cosmic fear is used by all religious systems. The image of God, the supreme ruler of the universe and its inhabitants, is moulded out of the familiar emotion of fear of vulnerability and trembling in the face of impenetrable and irreparable uncertainty; and then religion justifies itself through the role of effective mediator, an intercessor who pleads on behalf of the vulnerable and the frightened, at the sole court that can decree away the random blows of fate. Religion derives its power over human souls by brandishing the promise of security. But in order to do that, religion had first to reprocess the universe into God – by forcing it to speak . . .

In its original, spontaneously born form the cosmic prototype is a fear of an *anonymous* and *numb* force. The universe frightens, but does not speak. It demands nothing. It gives no instructions on how to proceed. It could not care less what the frightened, vulnerable humans would do or would refrain from doing. There is no point in talking to the starry heavens, mountains or sea. They would not hear, and they would not listen if they heard, let alone answer. There is no point in asking their forgiveness or favours. They would not care. Besides, despite all their tremendous might, they could not abide by the penitents' wishes even if they cared; they lack not just eyes, ears, minds and hearts, but also the ability to choose and the power of discretion, and so also the ability to act on their will and to accelerate or slow down, arrest or reverse what would have happened anyway. Their moves are inscrutable to human weaklings, but also to themselves. They are, as the biblical God said at the beginning of His conversation with Moses, 'what they are' – but they would not be able to say that – no point in asking them . . .

The frightening universe turned into a frightening God when the word had been spoken (John's Gospel got it right, after all . . .). The point is, though, that although the wondrous transformation of the universe into God reforged frightened beings into slaves of Divine commands, it was also the act of an oblique human empowerment. From now on, humans had to be docile, submissive and compliant – but they could also, at least in principle, do something to make sure that the awesome catastrophes they feared would pass them by. Now they could gain nights free of nightmares in exchange for days filled with acquiescence.

'There were thunders and lightnings, and a thick cloud upon the mount . . . and the whole mount quaked greatly' 'so that all the people that was in the camp trembled'. But among all that blood-curdling and mind-boggling turmoil and racket, the voice of God had been heard: 'Now therefore, if ye will obey my voice indeed, and keep my covenant, then ye shall be a peculiar treasure unto me above all people.' 'And all the people answered together, and said, All that the Lord hath spoken we will do' (Exodus 19). Obviously pleased with their oath of unswerving obedience, God promised the people to lead them 'unto a land flowing with milk and honey' (Exodus 33).

One can see that, if it is meant to be, as Bakhtin suggested, a story of the cosmic fear recycled into the 'official' kind, it seems so far to be either unsatisfactory or incomplete. It has told us that starting from the memorable Sinai encounter people came to be restrained in whatever they did from then on by a code of law (spelled out in meticulous detail once they signed a blank cheque promising to obey God's wishes whatever those wishes might be). But it has told us as well, though not in so many words, that God – now the source of 'official' fear – must have been from that moment on similarly bound: by his people's obedience. God had acquired will and discretion only to surrender them again! By the simple expedient of being docile, people could oblige God to be benevolent. Humans thereby acquired a patented medicine against vulnerability, and a foolproof way to exorcise the spectre of uncertainty. Providing they observed the Law to the letter, they would be neither vulnerable nor tormented by uncertainty. But without vulnerability and uncertainty, there would be no fear; and without fear, no power . . .

And so to account for the origins of an 'official' power that matches the awesome might of the 'cosmic' pattern the Exodus story must be complemented. And it was – by the Book of Job. That book made the signing of the Mount Sinai covenant enforceable in only one direction through being made amenable to a unilateral cancellation.

For the denizens of a modern state conceived as a *Rechtstaat* the story of Job was all but incomprehensible; it went against the grain of what they were trained to believe the harmony and the logic of life was about. To philosophers the story of Job was a continuous and incurable headache; it dashed their hopes of discovering, or inserting, logic and harmony in the chaotic flow of events called 'history'. Generations of theologians broke their teeth trying in vain to gnaw at its mystery: like the rest of modern men and women (and everyone who memorized the message of the Book of Exodus) they were taught to seek a rule and a norm, but the message of the book was that *there is no rule and no norm*; more exactly, no rule or norm that the supreme power is bound by. The Book of Job anticipates the later Carl Schmitt's blunt verdict that 'the sovereign is he who has the power of exemption.'

What the Book of Job proclaims is that God owes His worshippers nothing – certainly not an account of His actions. God's omnipotence includes the power of caprice and whim, the power to make miracles and to ignore the logic of necessity that lesser beings have no choice but to obey. God may strike at will, and if He refrains from striking, it is only because this is His (good, benign, benevolent, loving) will. The idea that humans may control God's action by whatever means, including the meek and faithful following of His commands and sticking to the letter of the Divine Law, is a blasphemy.

Unlike the numb universe that He replaced, God speaks and gives commands. With the ability to command comes however a limitation: he who speaks also hears and can listen . . . God hears what the humans think and want, and He may find out whether commands have been obeyed so that the obstreperous may be punished. Unlike the numb and dumb universe, God is *not indifferent* to what human weaklings think and do. But *like* the universe He replaced, He is *not bound* by what humans think or do. He can *make exceptions* – and the logics of consistency or universality are not exempt from that Divine prerogative. The power to exempt simultaneously founds God's absolute power and the human's continuing, incurable fear. Thanks to that power of exemption, humans are, as they were in the pre-Law times, vulnerable and uncertain.

If this is what human power is about (and it is), and if this is how power extracts the lodes of discipline on which it relies (and it does), then the *production* of 'official fear' is the key to the power's effectiveness. Cosmic fear may need no human mediators; official fear, like all other artifices, cannot do without them. Official fear can be only *contrived*. Earthly powers do not come to the rescue of humans already gripped by fear – though they try everything possible, and more, to convince their subjects that this is indeed the case. Earthly powers, much like the novelties of consumer markets, must create their own demand. For their grip to hold, their objects must be *made*, and *kept*, vulnerable and insecure.

And they are made, and kept. Reflecting on the message of Franz Kafka's allegory of the subterranean shelter which an unnamed safety-obsessed animal spent its life designing, digging and endlessly perfecting only to deepen the terror that kept it working,[13] Siegfried Kracauer suggests that in human societies

> the building that one generation after another constructs is sinister, because this structure is to guarantee a security that men cannot attain. The more systematically they plan it, the less they are able to breathe in it; the more seamlessly they try to erect it, the more inevitably it becomes a dungeon . . .
>
> Since this fear also wants to eliminate (the) insecurities inherent to creaturely existence, the burrow is a work of self-deception.[14]

He concludes: 'The measures provoked by existential fear are themselves a threat to existence.' Like the mysterious mole psychoanalysed by Kafka, earthly powers feeding on 'insecurities inherent to human existence' dedicate their labours to the creation of threats against which they will later promise to protect – and the more successful they are in their creative work the larger and more intense grows the demand for protection.

When everyone, at all times, is vulnerable and uncertain as to what the next morning may bring, it is survival and safety, not a sudden catastrophe, that appear to be the exception – indeed a miracle that defies an ordinary human's comprehension and requires superhuman foresight, wisdom and acting powers to be performed. It is the *avoidance* of the randomly distributed blows that appears to be an exemption, an exceptional gift, a show of grace, a proof of the wisdom and effectiveness of emergency measures, heightened vigilance, extraordinary efforts and exceptionally shrewd precautions.

Human vulnerability and uncertainty are the principal raison d'être of all political power; and all political power must attend to a regular renewal of its credentials.

In an average modern society, vulnerability and insecurity of existence and the necessity of pursuing life purposes under conditions of acute and unredeemable uncertainty are assured by the exposure of life pursuits to market forces. Apart from putting in place, monitoring and guarding the legal conditions of market freedoms, political power has no need to interfere any further in securing a sufficient quantity and permanent supply of 'official fear'. In demanding subjects' discipline and law observance, it may rest its legitimacy on the promise to mitigate the extent of the already existing vulnerability and uncertainty of its citizens: to limit harms and damages perpetrated by the free play of market forces, to shield the vulnerable against excessively painful blows and to insure the uncertain against the risks that free competition necessarily entails. Such legitimation found its ultimate expression in the self-definition of the modern form of government as a 'welfare state'.

The idea of the 'welfare state' (more to the point, as Robert Castel suggests, 'the social state'[15] – a state bent on fighting back and neutralizing socially produced dangers to individual and collective existence) declared the intention to 'socialize' individual risks and to make their reduction the task and responsibility of the state. Submission to state power was to be legitimized by its endorsement of an insurance policy against individual mischance and calamity.

That formula of political power is presently receding into the past. 'Welfare state' institutions are being progressively dismantled and phased out, while restraints previously imposed on business activities and on the free play of market competition and its consequences are removed. The protective functions of the state are being tapered to embrace a small minority of the unemployable and invalid, though even that minority tends to be reclassified from the issue of social care into the issue of law and order: an incapacity to participate in the market game tends to be increasingly criminalized. The state washes its hands of the vulnerability and uncertainty arising from the logic (or illogicality) of the free market, now redefined as a private affair, a matter for individuals to deal with and cope with by the resources in their private possession. As Ulrich Beck put it, individuals are now expected to seek biographical solutions to systemic contradictions.[16]

These new trends have a side-effect: they sap the foundations on which state power, claiming a crucial role in fighting the vulnerability and uncertainty haunting its subjects, increasingly rested in modern times. The widely noted growth of political apathy, the loss of political interest and commitment ('no more salvation by society', as Peter Drucker famously put it), a growing disregard for law, multiplying signs of civic (and not-so-civic) disobedience, and last though not least, a massive retreat of the population from participation in institutionalized politics, all testify to the crumbling of the established foundations of state power.

Having rescinded or severely curtailed its past programmatic interference with market-produced insecurity, having proclaimed the perpetuation and intensification of that insecurity to be, on the contrary, the prime purpose and a duty of all political power dedicated to the well-being of its subjects, the contemporary state must seek other, non-economic varieties of vulnerability and uncertainty on which to rest its legitimacy. That alternative seems to have been recently located (and practised perhaps most spectacularly by the US administration, but as an exercise in pattern-setting and 'leading the way' rather than as an exception) in the issue of *personal safety*: threats and fears to human bodies, possessions and habitats arising from criminal activities, the anti-social conduct of the 'underclass' and, most recently, global terrorism.

Unlike the insecurity born of the market, which is if anything all too visible and obvious for comfort, that alternative insecurity with which it is hoped to restore the state's lost monopoly of redemption must be artificially beefed up, or at least highly dramatized to inspire a volume of 'official fear' sufficiently large to overshadow and relegate to a secondary position the worries about economically generated insecurity about which the state administration can do – and wishes to do – nothing. Unlike in the case of market-generated threats to livelihood and welfare, the extent of dangers to personal safety must be intensely advertised and painted in the darkest of colours, so that the non-materialization of threats can be applauded as an extraordinary event, a result of the vigilance, care and good-will of state organs.

As I write these words, trusted Washington authorities keep lifting the level of official alert and with dull regularity warn that 'another attack on the scale of September 11' is imminent, though no one can tell when and where and how it will happen. Americans are being advised to buy and store duct tape, plastic sheeting, three days' supplies of fresh water and a battery-powered radio. There has already been a run on the shops, and the larders and garden sheds are bursting with the DIY defences against the fallout from the global frontier-land.

The officially inspired and whipped-up fears play on the same human weaknesses that underlie Bakhtin's 'cosmic fear'. Professor

Robert Edelmann, introduced by the *Observer* health columnist Anna More as 'a consultant psychologist specialising in anxiety disorder', points to the way lack of control and ignorance merge and blend into a nerve-breaking uncertainty, brought about by the state-initiated and sponsored publicity given to risks and dangers; how the uncertainty and the anxiety it begets have been noted to result in widespread bouts of 'stress, sleeplessness and depression' that 'occur simultaneously with a sharp rise in sales of alcohol and cigarettes'. 'If we're driving our car at 100 mph, we assume we are in control, but you can't prepare for a terrorist attack.' The well-informed sources which have access to the information that'll never reach you, and all the information there is, admit frankly, and loudly, their ignorance of the terrorists' numbers, location and plans and announce that predicting the time and place of the next attack is out of the question. As Edelmann sums up: measured against billions of people apparently threatened by terrorist exploits, 'the numbers who are killed by terrorist activity is very small. If the government and the media put the same emphasis on the number of people killed each day on the road, we might be too petrified to get into our cars.'[17]

But 'making people uncertain and anxious' has been the task with which the CIA and FBI have been mostly occupied in recent months: warning the Americans of the imminent attempts on their safety that will most certainly be perpetrated though it is impossible to say where, when and against whom, putting them in a state of constant alert and so building up tension. There must be tension, the more of it the better, available for being relieved when the attempts do not occur – so that all credit for the relief may be ascribed by popular consent to the organs of law and order to which the state administration and its officially declared responsibilities are progressively reduced.

To its recent survey of Britain's most widely read dailies the *Guardian* (of 24 Jan. 2003) gave the heading: 'Press whips up asylum hysteria. Editors dub Britain a gangsters' heaven as they make direct links between refugees and terrorists.' While the British Prime Minister uses every public appearance to warn listeners that a terrorist assault on Britain is certain, though its place and time are uncertainty incarnate, and his Home Secretary compares British society to a 'coiled spring' because of its seething

and festering asylum-seeker problems, tabloids are quick to link
and blend the two warnings into an asylum/terrorist hysteria.
Though not just the tabloids, to be sure. As Stephen Castles has
observed, 'following the events of 11 September 2001, refugees
have been branded as a sinister transnational threat to national
security – even though none of the 11 September terrorists were
actually refugees or asylum seekers.'[18]

Were there a competition for the best composite political
formula for the current edition of officially endorsed fear, the first
prize would probably go to the *Sun* – for a phrase that in addition to being eminently easy to ingest leaves nothing to guesswork
or the imagination: 'We have an open invitation to terrorists to
live off our benefits.' A masterstroke indeed. The novel fear of the
terrorists merged and cemented with the already well-entrenched,
but constantly in need of new food, hatred of 'spongers', killing
two birds with one stone and arming the ongoing crusade against
'welfare scroungers' with a new, indomitable weapon of mass
intimidation. While economic uncertainty is no longer attended
to by a state that would rather leave it to individual subjects
to individually seek individual cures for individual existential
insecurity, the new brand of officially inspired and whipped-up
collective fear has been enlisted in the service of the political
formula. The citizens' concerns with personal well-being have
thereby been shifted away from the treacherous ground of
market-promoted *precarité* on to which state governments have
neither the capacity nor the will to tread, and towards a safer
and much more tele-photogenic area, where the awesome might
and steely resolution of the rulers can be effectively displayed
for public admiration.

Other tabloids promptly fell in line, hotly contesting priority
in unmasking the sinister connection of asylum seekers with
terrorist conspiracy (the *Daily Express* reproduced twenty of its
past front pages with the triumphant conclusion, 'We told you
so!') and composing ever new variants of the choral motif, vying
for the most shrilling notes and the highest pitches (the *Daily Mail*
suggested that 'had Hitler come to Britain in 1944 he would have
been entitled to asylum'). As Steven Morris, the author of the
Guardian survey, noted, the *News of the World* 'placed a column

from David Blunkett warning about the myths surrounding refugees and terrorism opposite a report about the asylum seekers who live near the spot where DC Oake died' (DC Oake was shot in the course of arresting an immigrant suspect). Indeed, no 't' has been left uncrossed, nor was any 'i' left without a dot. As Fazil Kawani, the communications director of the Refugee Council condensed the overall message: 'These reports give the impression that all asylum seekers are terrorists and criminals.' In a bizarre mixture of clichés drawn from mutually incompatible value universes, the *Sun* (in its editorial of 27 Jan. 2003) expounds: 'This sea of humanity is polluted with terrorism and disease and threatens our way of life . . . Blair must say *no more now*, revoke the human rights law *now* and lock up all the illegals *now* until they can be checked.' Perhaps envious of the copy-selling records of such alarms, the respectable and respected *Guardian* (of 5 Feb. 2003) resorted to the vocabulary of butcher shops and in a first-page banner proclaimed a 'plan to slash asylum numbers'. Slash . . . Do you smell blood?

In his thorough study of the genealogy of modern fears, Philippe Robert found out that starting from the early years of the twentieth century (that is, by more than a sheer coincidence, from the early years of the social state), fears of crime began to subside. They went on diminishing until the middle 1970s, when a sudden eruption of 'personal safety' panic focused in France on the crime apparently brewing in the *banlieues* where immigrant settlers were concentrated. What erupted was however, in Robert's view, but a 'delayed action bomb': explosive security concerns had already been stored up by the slow yet steady phasing out of the collective insurance that the social state used to offer and by the rapid deregulation of the labour market. Recast as a 'danger to safety', the immigrants offered a convenient alternative focus for the apprehensions born of the sudden shakiness and vulnerability of social positions, and so they were a relatively safer outlet for the discharge of anxiety and anger which such apprehensions could not but cause.[19]

In Hans-Jörg Albrecht's view, it is only the link between immigration and public disquiet about rising violence and fears for security that is novel; otherwise nothing much has changed since the beginning of the modern state – the folkloristic images of devils and demons that used to 'soak up' diffuse security fears in the past 'have been transformed into danger and risks'.

> Demonisation has been replaced by the concept and the strategy of 'dangerisation'. Political governance, therefore, has become partially dependent on the deviant other and the mobilisation of feelings of safety. Political power, and its establishment, as well as its preservation, are today dependent on carefully selected campaign issues, among which safety (and feelings of unsafety) is paramount.[20]

Immigrants, let us note, fit better into such a purpose than any other category of genuine or putative villains. There is a sort of 'elective affinity' between immigrants (that human waste of distant parts of the globe unloaded into 'our own backyard') and the least bearable of our own, home-grown fears. When all places and positions feel shaky and are deemed no longer reliable, the sight of immigrants rubs salt into the wound. Immigrants, and particularly the fresh arrivals among them, exude the faint odour of the waste disposal tip which in its many disguises haunts the nights of the prospective casualties of rising vulnerability. For their detractors and haters, immigrants embody – visibly, tangibly, in the flesh – the inarticulate yet hurtful and painful presentiment of their own disposability. One is tempted to say that were there no immigrants knocking at the doors, they would have to be invented . . . Indeed, they provide governments with an ideal 'deviant other', a most welcome target for the 'carefully selected campaign issues'.

Stripped of a large part of their sovereign prerogatives and capacities by globalization forces which they are impotent to resist, let alone to control, governments have no choice but to 'carefully select' targets which they can (conceivably) overpower and against which they can aim their rhetorical salvos and flex their muscles while being heard and seen doing so by their grateful subjects. As Adam Crawford explains,

> 'community safety', in so far as it is concerned with 'quality of life' issues, is saturated with concerns about safety and 'ontological

insecurity'. It evokes a 'solution' to crime, incivility and disorder, thus enabling the (local) state to reassert some form of sovereignty. Symbolically, it reaffirms control of a given territory, which is visible and tangible . . . The current governmental preoccupation with petty crime, disorder and anti-social behaviour reflects a source of 'anxiety' about which something can be done in an otherwise uncertain world.[21]

And the (national, recast in the age of globalization into local) governments of our day are 'casting about for spheres of activity in which they can assert their sovereignty'[22] and demonstrate in public, convincingly, that they have done so.

Making associations may be murderous, particularly if they are hammered home with dull monotony and deafening loudness. They may also, for the same reasons, seem in time self-evident and no longer call for proof. Heeding Hume's warning, we may insist that *post hoc* (or *apud hoc*, for that matter) *non est propter hoc*[23] – but then Hume suggested that assuming the opposite of that truth is a most common fallacy and one most difficult to eradicate. Overgeneral, unwarranted or even fanciful as the association of terrorists with asylum seekers and 'economic migrants' might have been, it did its job: the figure of the 'asylum seeker', once prompting human compassion and spurring an urge to help, has been sullied and defiled, while the very idea of 'asylum', once a matter of civil and civilized pride, has been reclassified as a dreadful concoction of shameful naivety and criminal irresponsibility. As to the 'economic migrants' who have retreated from the headlines to give room for the sinister, poison-brewing and disease-carrying 'asylum seekers', it did not help their image that they embody, as Jelle van Buuren has pointed out,[24] everything that the dominant neoliberal creed holds sacred and promotes as the precepts that should rule everyone's conduct (that is, 'the desire for progress and prosperity, individual responsibility, readiness to take risks, etc.'). Already accused of 'sponging' and sticking to their wicked and disreputable habits and creeds, they could not now, however hard they tried, shake off the wholesale charge of terrorist conspiracy stuck to 'people like them', the flotsam and jetsam of the planetary tides of human waste. This, as already alluded to above, is the new use to which wasted humans, and particularly those wasted humans who have managed to land on affluent shores, have been put.

A diligent watcher of TV and reader of newspapers would probably have noted by now that while asylum seekers, alongside terrorists, command most of the front-page headlines and lead items of the news, 'economic migrants' have virtually vanished from public exposure; and that in all the excitement surrounding the newly made-in-hell marriage of the first, the disappearance of the second went by and large unnoticed. One explanation is that while the call signal has changed, the sentiments and attitudes stirred up have not. The images of 'economic migrants' and of 'asylum seekers' both stand for 'wasted humans', and whichever of the two figures is used to arouse resentment and anger, the object of the resentment and the target on which the anger is to be unloaded remains much the same. The purpose of the exercise remains the same as well: to reinforce (salvage? build anew?) the mouldy and decaying walls meant to guard the hallowed distinction between the 'inside' and the 'outside' in a globalizing world that pays it little if any respect and routinely violates it.

The sole difference between the two kinds of 'wasted humans' is that while asylum seekers tend to be the products of successive instalments of order-designing and order-building zeal, economic migrants are a side-product of economic modernization, which, as already discussed, has by now embraced the totality of the planet. The origins of both kinds of 'human waste' are currently global, though in the absence of any global institutions able and willing to strike effectively at the roots of the problem, a furious search for locally manageable responses to the global waste disposal-and/or-recycling challenge should hardly come as a surprise.

There is one more useful function that human waste can perform to keep the world going as it is.

Refugees, the displaced, asylum seekers, migrants, the *sans papiers*, they are the waste of globalization. But they are not the only waste turned out in ever rising volumes in our times. There is also the 'traditional' industrial waste which accompanied modern production from the start. Its disposal presents problems no less formidable than the disposal of human waste, and ever more horrifying – and for much the same reasons: the economic progress that is spreading to the most remote nooks and crannies of the 'filled up' planet, trampling on its way all remaining forms of life alternative to consumer society.

Consumers in a consumer society, like the inhabitants of Calvino's Leonia, need rubbish collectors, and many of them, and of the sort who will not shun touching and handling what has already been confined to the rubbish heap – but the consumers are not willing to do the rubbish collectors' jobs themselves. After all, they have been groomed to enjoy things, not to suffer them. They have been educated to resent boredom, drudgery and tedious pastimes. They have been drilled to seek implements that do for them what they used to do themselves. They were tuned to the world of the ready-to-use and the world of instant satisfaction. This is what the delights of consumer life are all about. This is what consumerism is all about – and it certainly does not include the performance of dirty, gruelling, wearisome, or just unentertaining, 'no-fun' jobs. With each successive triumph of consumerism, the need for rubbish collectors grows, and the numbers of people willing to join their ranks shrinks.

People whose orthodox and forcibly devalued forms of making a living have already been earmarked for destruction, and who themselves have been assigned to disposable waste, cannot be choosers. In their night dreams they may fashion themselves in the likeness of consumers, but it is physical survival, not consumer revelry, that fills their days. The stage is set for the meeting of human rejects with the rejects of consumer feasts; indeed, they seem to have been made for each other . . . Behind the colourful curtain of free competition and equal trade, *homo hierarchicus* lingers. In the caste society, only untouchable people could (and had to) handle untouchable things. In the world of global freedom and equality, lands and population have been arranged in a hierarchy of castes.

Rachel Shabi quotes Jim Puckett, an environmental campaigner: 'Toxic waste will always run downhill on an economic path of least resistance.' In Guiyu, a Chinese village converted into an electronic junkyard, as in numerous other places in India, Vietnam, Singapore or Pakistan populated by former peasants who have fallen (or been thrown) overboard from the vehicle of economic progress, the electronic waste of the West is 'recycled'.

> Leftover plastics are either burned, creating piles of contaminated ash, or dumped along with other processing residues in rivers, along irrigation canals or in fields. It is primitive, dangerous work. Poisonous waste creeps into skin and lungs and seeps into the land and water. Guiyu's soil contains 200 times the level of lead considered hazardous; the drinking water is 2400 times over the World Health Authority lead threshold.[25]

In Britain we produce around 1 million tonnes of electronic waste every year and expect to double that quantity by 2010. Electronic utility goods, not so long ago counted among the most valuable and durable possessions, are now eminently disposable and meant to be disposed of, and fast. Marketing companies speed up their travel to obsolescence, 'constantly putting goods out of date, or creating the impression that if you don't keep up, you will' (be put out of date). As David Walker, managing director of an IT recycling company, complains, 'If you've got a low-end Pentium II or less, even the charities wouldn't want it.' No wonder that more and more humans degraded to the low-end level to which even the ailing national or inchoate global charities would not stoop are needed. And they are found, thanks to the co-operation of human-waste producing plants. In Guiyu, there are 100,000 of them – men, women and children working for the equivalent of 94p a day.

The above information has been gleaned from pages 36 and 39 of the *Guardian*'s glossy weekend supplement. Between those pages, there is a full-page advertisement for a seductively smart and shiny washing machine with a huge caption: 'If someone tells you there's a better washing machine than this they're lying.' Perhaps. But if someone tells you that the advertised machine (which, as stated in the advertisement, even remembers your favourite wash programs for you) is meant to remain your favourite long after a new and improved machine is advertised, they are also lying.

Not all industrial and household waste can however be transported to the far-away places where human waste may do, for a few pence, the hazardous and dirty job of waste disposal. One may try – and one does – to arrange the necessary meeting of material and human waste closer to home. According to Naomi Klein, the ever more popular solution (pioneered by the European Union but quickly followed by the United States) is a 'multi-tiered regional stronghold'.

> A fortress continent is a bloc of nations that joins forces to extract favourable trade terms from other countries, while patrolling their shared external borders to keep people from those countries out. But if a continent is serious about being a fortress, it also has to invite one or two poor countries within its walls, because somebody has to do the dirty work and heavy lifting.[26]

Fortress America – the North Atlantic Free Trade Area, the US internal market extended to incorporate Canada and Mexico ('after oil', Naomi Klein points out, 'immigrant labour is the fuel driving the southwest economy' of the US) – was supplemented in July 2001 by 'Plan Sur', according to which the Mexican government took responsibility for the massive policing of its southern boundary and for effectively stopping the tide of impoverished human waste flowing to the US from Latin American countries. Since then, hundreds of thousands of migrants have been stopped, incarcerated and deported by Mexican police before reaching US borders. As to Fortress Europe: 'Poland, Bulgaria, Hungary and the Czech Republic are the postmodern serfs, providing the low-wage factories where clothes, electronics and cars are produced for 20–25 per cent of the cost to make them in western Europe.' Inside fortress continents, 'a new social hierarchy' has been put in place in an attempt to find a balance between the two blatantly contradictory yet equally vital postulates of airtight borders and of access to cheap, undemanding, docile labour ready to accept and do whatever is on offer; or of free trade and the need to pander to anti-immigrant sentiments. 'How do you stay open to business and closed to people?' asks Klein. And answers: 'Easy. First you expand the perimeter. Then you lock down.'

3

To each waste its dumping site

Or the waste of globalization

Several functions have been discussed that are currently performed by the human casualties of the planet-wide victory of
economic progress. Circling the globe in search of sustenance and
attempting to settle where sustenance can be found, they offer an
easy target for unloading anxieties prompted by the widespread
fears of social redundancy; in the process, they are enlisted to help
in the efforts of state governments to reassert their impaired and
weakening authority. Other useful services into which they are
drawn have also been named, albeit briefly. It has been suggested
that between them, such 'latent functions' (as Robert Merton
could call them) make an effective solution to the 'problem of
migrants' all but impossible.

One more function has been scrutinized by François de
Bernard. A most spectacular and potentially sinister consequence
of the erratic globalizing processes, uncontrolled and running wild
as they have been thus far, is in his view the progressive 'crimi-
nalization of the globe and globalization of crime'.[1] A consider-
able part of the billions of dollars, pounds and euros that change
hands daily come from criminal sources and are destined for criminal sources. 'Never before were the mafias so numerous, powerful, well armed and prosperous.' Most political powers most of
the time are unable and unwilling to engage in combat with
criminal forces which all too often command resources none of
the governments, singly and sometimes jointly, can match. This is
one of the reasons why, in Bernard's view, governments prefer to
unleash popular animosity against petty crime than to engage in

the battles that are likely to drag on without end, being certain to draw on incalculable resources though virtually bound to be lost. Seeking Public Enemy Number One among the hapless immigrants of the *banlieues* and asylum seekers' camps is considerably more opportune and expedient, but above all less troublesome. With more effect and less expense, the immigrant districts teeming with prospective pickpockets and muggers can be used as the battlefield of the great war for law and order which governments wage with great vigour and even greater publicity, while not being averse to 'subsidiarizing' and subletting to private security outlets and citizens' initiatives.

The exact spread and depth of the power of mafias and the precise volume of criminal deals is exceedingly difficult, perhaps impossible, to assess. The reason is simple enough: though the insidiousness and precision of the equipment which a 'Big Brother' could deploy 'to watch you' have risen enormously since Orwell's times, no 'Big Brother' is watching the global space in which mafias operate and in which they can always hide if need be. That space, eminently extraterritorial by the standards of territoriality still enforced and observed in the allocation and claiming of political sovereignty, is essentially a 'politics-free area'. As Richard Rorty observed in 1996, the 'central fact of globalization' is that

> The economic situation of the citizens of a nation state has passed beyond the control of the laws of the state . . . [T]here is no way in which the laws of Brazil or the US can dictate that money earned in the country will be spent in the country, or money saved in the country invested in the country. . . . We now have a global over-class which makes all the major economic decisions, and makes them in entire independence of the legislatures, and *a fortiori* of the will of the voters, of any given country . . . The absence of a global polity means that the super-rich can operate without any thought of any interests save their own.[2]

If this is however the 'central fact of globalization', then the genuine issue is not so much the 'globalization of crime', as de Bernard suggests, but the annulment of the distinction between 'legal' and 'illegal' which only an abiding and enforceable law may draw. There is no such global law to violate. There is no global law in operation that could permit the setting apart of mafia-style criminal pursuits from 'normal business activity'. And there is no global polity of any shape or form that would be able to do so much as to postulate the introduction of globally binding rules of the game, let alone attempt to make them indeed binding. In the global space, rules are set and abandoned in the course of action, and it is the stronger, the craftier, the quicker, the more resourceful and less scrupulous who make them stick and get unstuck. In the global 'space of flows' (Manuel Castells's expression) the concept of law can only be deployed following Jacques Derrida's injunction of using it *sous rupture*. Quoting Teubner and Böckenförde,[3] Hauke Brunkhorst points out that that strange 'global law', unlike the law we have grown to expect in the practices of modern nation-states, is 'far removed from politics, without a constitutional form, without democracy, without hierarchy from below, without an unbroken chain of democratic legitimation'. It is 'rule without a ruler'. Whatever may be passing as a 'global law' 'cannot be utilized in a court of law, and only in the rarest of cases can it be enforced. In a way comparable to old Roman civil law, the enforcement of international law is at the will of those who have the *power* to enforce it.'[4]

All the others – lesser partners and minor players – have no choice but to curry favour with the powerful. At best, the global 'legal system' is made up of patronage and clientele and currently presents (in deed if not in theory) a patchwork of privileges and deprivations. It is the most powerful players that distribute, sparingly and with an eye on the preservation of their monopoly, the right to seek the law's protection. It is not that the global mafias operate in the seams between legal structures monitored and serviced by nation-states: it is rather that once freed from effective legal constraints and depending solely on the current power differential, all operations in the global space follow (by design or by default) the pattern heretofore associated with mafias or mafia-style corruption of the rule of law.

Hence the anxiety – spurred by the painful experience of being lost and hapless: we are not the only ones, *no one* is in control, no one is in the know. There is no telling when and from where the

next blow will strike, how far its ripples will reach and how lethal
the cataclysm will be. Uncertainty and anguish born of uncertainty
are globalization's staple products. State powers can do next to
nothing to placate, let alone quash uncertainty. The most they can
do is to refocus it on objects within reach; shift it from the objects
they can do nothing about to those they can at least make a show
of being able to handle and control. Refugees, asylum seekers,
immigrants – the waste products of globalization – fit the bill
perfectly.

As I argued elsewhere,[5] refugees and immigrants, coming from
'far away' yet making a bid to settle in the neighbourhood, are
uniquely suitable for the role of the effigy to be burnt as the
spectre of 'global forces', feared and resented for doing their job
without consulting those whom its outcome is bound to affect.
After all, asylum seekers and 'economic migrants' are collective
replicas (an alter ego? fellow travellers? mirror-images? carica-
tures?) of the new power elite of the globalized world, widely
(and with reason) suspected to be the true villain of the piece.
Like that elite, they are untied to any place, shifty, unpredictable. Like that elite, they epitomize the unfathomable 'space
of flows' where the roots of the present-day precariousness of the
human condition are sunk. Seeking in vain for other, more adequate outlets, fears and anxieties rub off on targets close to hand
and re-emerge as popular resentment and fear of the 'aliens
nearby'. Uncertainty cannot be defused or dispersed in a direct
confrontation with the other embodiment of extraterritoriality:
the global elite drifting beyond the reach of human control. That
elite is much too powerful to be confronted and challenged point-
blank, even if its exact location was known (which it is not).
Refugees, on the other hand, are a clearly visible, and sitting, target
for the surplus anguish.

Let me add that when faced with an influx of 'outsiders', the
waste of the planet-wide triumph of modernity but also of a new
planet-wide disorder in the making, 'the established' (to deploy
Norbert Elias's memorable terms) have every reason to feel
threatened. In addition to representing the 'great unknown' which
all 'strangers in our midst' embody, these particular outsiders, the

refugees, bring home distant noises of war and the stench of gutted homes and scorched villages that cannot but remind the settled how easily the cocoon of their safe and familiar (safe *because* familiar) routine may be pierced or crushed and how deceptive the security of their settlement must be. The refugee, as Bertolt Brecht pointed out in *Die Landschaft des Exils*, is 'ein Bote des Unglücks' ('a harbinger of ill tidings').

With the benefit of hindsight, we can see that there was a genuine watershed in modern history in the decade separating the 'glorious thirty years' of postwar reconstruction, of social compact and of the developmental optimism that accompanied the dismantling of the colonial system and the mushrooming of 'new nations', from the brave new world of erased or punctured boundaries, information deluge, rampant globalization, a consumer feast in the affluent North and a 'deepening sense of desperation and exclusion in a large part of the rest of the world' arising from 'the spectacle of wealth on the one hand and destitution on the other'.[6] During that decade, the setting in which men and women face up to life challenges was surreptitiously yet radically transformed, invalidating extant life wisdoms and calling for a thorough revision and overhaul of life strategies.

We have not as yet fathomed the full depths of that great transformation. Not for lack of trying: given how short a distance away it is in time, it is advisable to view all findings and judgements as partial and all syntheses as provisional. With the passage of time, successive layers of emergent realities come into view, each calling for a deeper and more comprehensive revision of received beliefs and our conceptual net than was required by the one before in order for it to be scanned and its significance revealed. We haven't reached the bottom layer yet; even if we did, though, we wouldn't be able to decide for sure that we had.

One fateful aspect of the transformation was revealed relatively early and since then it has been thoroughly documented: the passage from a 'social state' model of inclusive community to a 'criminal justice', 'penal', or 'crime control', exclusionary state. David Garland, for instance, observes that:

there has been a marked shift of emphasis from the welfare to
the penal modality ... The penal mode, as well as becoming
more prominent, has become more punitive, more expressive, more
security-minded ... The welfare mode, as well as becoming
more muted, has become more conditional, more offence-centred,
more risk conscious ...

The offenders ... are now less likely to be represented in official discourse as socially deprived citizens in need of support. They
are depicted instead as culpable, undeserving and somewhat dangerous individuals.[7]

Loïc Wacquant notes a 'redefinition of the state's mission'; the
state 'retreats from the economic arena, asserts the necessity to
reduce its social role to the widening and strengthening of its penal
intervention'.[8]

Ulf Hedetoft describes the same aspect of the transformation
of two to three decades ago from a different angle (or perhaps
another, but intimately related aspect of the same). He notes that
'borders are being redrawn between Us and Them more rigidly'
than ever before. Following Andreas and Snyder,[9] Hedetoft suggests that in addition to becoming more selective, bloated, diversified and diffuse in their assumed forms, borders have turned into
what could be called 'asymmetric membranes' that allow exit but
'protect against unwanted entrance of units from the other side'.

Stepping up control measures at the external borders, but just as
importantly a tighter visa-issuing regime in countries of emigration
in 'the South' ... [Borders] have diversified, as have border controls, taking place not just at the conventional places ... but in airports, at embassies and consulates, at asylum centres, and in virtual
space in the form of stepped-up collaboration between police and
immigration authorities in different countries.[10]

As if in order to supply immediate evidence for Hedetoft's
thesis, the British Prime Minister Tony Blair received Ruud
Lubbers, the UN High Commissioner for Refugees, to suggest the
establishment of 'safe havens' for prospective asylum seekers *near
their homes*, that is at a safe distance from Britain and the other
well-off countries that were until recently their natural destina-

tions. In the typical newspeak of the post-Great Transformation era, Home Secretary David Blunkett described the topic of the Blair/Lubbers conversation as 'new challenges for developed countries posed by those who use the asylum system as a route to the West' (using that newspeak, one could complain, for instance, of the challenge for settled people from shipwrecked sailors who use the rescue system as a route to dry land).

Perhaps the two trends signalled here are but two related manifestations of the same enhanced, well-nigh obsessive concern with security; perhaps they both can be explained by a shift in the balance between the inclusivist and exclusionary tendencies that are perpetually present; or perhaps they are mutually unrelated phenomena, each subject to its own logic. It can be shown however that whatever their immediate causes, both trends derive from the same root: *the global spread of the modern way of life, which by now has reached the furthest limits of the planet.* It has cancelled the division between 'centre' and 'periphery', or more correctly between 'modern' (or 'developed') and 'premodern' (or 'underdeveloped' or 'backward') forms of life – a division that accompanied the greater part of modern history, when the modern overhaul of received ways was confined to a relatively narrow, though constantly expanding sector of the globe. As long as it remained relatively narrow, that sector could use the resulting power differential as a safety valve protecting it from overheating, and the rest of the planet as a dumping site for the toxic waste of its own continuous modernization.

The planet, however, is now full. That means, among other things, that typically modern processes such as order-building and economic progress take place everywhere and so everywhere 'human waste' is produced and turned out in ever rising quantities – this time, however, in the absence of 'natural' refuse tips suitable for its storage and potential recycling. The process first anticipated by Rosa Luxemburg a century ago (though described by her in mainly economic, rather than explicitly social terms) has reached its ultimate limit.

Rosa Luxemburg, let us recall, suggested that though capitalism 'needs non-capitalist social organizations as the setting for its development', 'it proceeds by assimilating the very condition

which alone can ensure its own existence': 'Non-capitalist organizations provide a fertile soil for capitalism: capital feeds on the
ruins of such organizations, and although this non-capitalist *milieu*
is indispensable for accumulation, the latter proceeds at the cost
of this medium nevertheless, by eating it up.'[11]

A snake feeding on its own tail . . . Or we could say, reaching
for a term invented quite recently, that – when the distance
between the tail and the stomach has become too short for the
snake's chances of survival and the self-destructive prospects of
the feast become evident – the 'asset stripping' that needs ever
new assets to be stripped must sooner or later exhaust its supplies
or reduce them below the level required for its own sustenance.

Rosa Luxemburg envisaged a capitalism dying for the lack of
food – collapsing through eating up the last meadow of 'other-
ness' on which it grazed. A hundred years later it seems that a
most fatal, possibly *the* most fatal, result of modernity's global
triumph is the acute crisis of the human-waste disposal industry:
with the volume of human waste outgrowing the extant manage-
rial capacity, there is a plausible prospect of the now planetary
modernity choking on its own waste products which it can neither
reassimilate nor annihilate. There are numerous signals of the
fast-rising toxicity of the rapidly accumulating waste. The morbid
consequences of industrial and household waste for the planet's
ecological balance and capacity for support have been a matter of
intense concern for some time now (though not much action has
followed the debates); we have not however arrived anywhere
near to seeing clearly and grasping in full the far-reaching effects
of the growing masses of 'wasted humans' on the political balance
and social equilibrium of human planetary coexistence.

The new 'fullness of the planet' – the global reach of modernization and so the planetary spread of the modern mode of life – has
two direct consequences briefly signalled before.

The first consequence is the blockage of outlets that in the past
allowed a regular and timely draining and cleansing of the relatively few modern enclaves of the planet of their surplus waste
(that is, the excess of waste over the capacity of recycling outfits)
which the modern way of life could not but have produced on an

ever rising scale. Once the modern mode of life stopped being a privilege of selected lands, the primary outlets for human-waste disposal, that is the 'empty' or 'no man's' territories (more precisely, the territories that thanks to the global power differential could be seen and treated as void and/or masterless), have vanished. For the 'redundant humans' now turned out in the parts of planet that have recently jumped into or fallen under the juggernaut of modernity, such outlets were never in existence; in the so-called 'premodern' societies, innocent of the problem of waste, human or non-human alike, the need for them did not arise. As an effect of that blocking or non-provision of external outlets, societies increasingly turn the sharp edge of exclusionary practices against themselves.

If the excess of population (that is, the part that cannot be reassimilated into normal life patterns and reprocessed back into the category of 'useful' members of society) can be routinely removed and transported beyond the boundaries of the enclosure within which an economic balance and social equilibrium are sought, people who escape transportation and remain inside the enclosure, even if currently redundant, are earmarked for recycling. They are 'out', but only temporarily – their 'staying out' is an abnormality that commands and musters a cure; they clearly need to be helped 'back in' as soon as possible. They are the 'reserve army of labour' and must be put in and held in such a shape as would allow them to return to active service at the first opportunity.

All that changes, however, once the channels for draining human surplus are blocked. As the 'redundant' population stays inside and rubs shoulders with the 'useful' and 'legitimate' rest, the line separating a transient incapacitation from the peremptory and final consignment to waste tends to be blurred and no longer legible. Rather than remaining as before a problem of a separate part of the population, assignment to 'waste' becomes everybody's potential prospect – one of the two poles between which everybody's present and future social standing oscillates. To deal with the 'problem of waste' in this new form the habitual tools and stratagems of intervention do not suffice; nor are they particularly adequate. The new policies soon to be invented in response to the

new shape of the old problem will most probably start by sub-
suming the policies once designed to deal with the problem in its
old shape. To be on the safe side, emergency measures aimed at
the issue of 'waste inside' will be preferred and sooner or later
given priority over all other modes of intervention in the issues of
redundancy as such, temporary or not.

All these and similar setbacks and reverses of fortune tend to
be magnified and made yet more acute in those parts of the globe
that have only recently been confronted with the previously
unknown phenomenon of 'surplus population' and the problem
of its disposal. 'Recently' in this case means belatedly – at a time
when the planet is already full, when no 'empty lands' are left to
serve as waste-disposal sites and when any asymmetry of boundaries is turned firmly against newcomers to the family of moderns.
Surrounding lands will not invite their surplus nor can be, as they
themselves were in the past, forced to accept and accommodate
it. Such 'latecomers to modernity' are left to seek a *local* solution
to a globally caused problem – though with meagre chances of
success.

Where family and communal businesses were once able and
willing to absorb, employ and support all newly born humans, and
at most times secure their survival, the surrender to global pressures and the laying of their own territory open to the unfettered
circulation of capital and commodities made them unviable. Only
now do the newcomers to the company of moderns experience
that separation of business from households which the pioneers
of modernity went through hundreds of years ago, with all its
attendant social upheavals and human misery but also with the
luxury of global solutions to locally produced problems – an abun-
dance of 'empty' and 'no man's lands' that could easily be used
to deposit the surplus population no longer absorbed by the
economy emancipated from familial and communal constraints: a
luxury not available to the latecomers.

Tribal wars and massacres, a proliferation of 'guerrilla armies'
(often little more than barely disguised bandit gangs) busy deci-
mating each other's ranks yet absorbing and annihilating the
'population surplus' (mostly the young, unemployable at home
and without prospects) in the process – in short, a 'neighbourhood
colonialism' or 'poor man's imperialism' – are among such 'local

solutions to global problems' the 'latecomers to modernity' are forced to deploy or rather have found themselves deploying. Hundreds of thousands of people are chased away from their homes, murdered or forced to run for life outside the borders of their country.

Perhaps the sole thriving industry in the lands of the latecomers (deviously and deceitfully dubbed 'developing countries') is the mass production of refugees. It is the ever more prolific products of that industry which the British Prime Minister proposes to unload 'near their home countries', in permanently temporary camps (deviously and deceitfully dubbed 'safe havens'), thereby exacerbating the already unmanageable 'surplus population' problems of immediate neighbours who willy-nilly run a similar industry. The aim is to keep 'local problems' local and so nip in the bud all attempts of latecomers to follow the example of the pioneers of modernity by seeking global (and the sole effective) solutions for locally manufactured problems. As I write these words, in another variation of the same theme NATO has been asked to mobilize its armies to help Turkey to seal its border with Iraq in view of the impending assault on the country. Many a statesperson of the pioneer countries objected, raising many imaginative reservations – but none mentioned publicly that the danger against which Turkey was to be protected was the influx of freshly-made-homeless Iraqi refugees, not an attack by battered and pulverized Iraqi soldiers.[12]

However earnest, the efforts to stem the tide of 'economic migration' are not and probably cannot be made a hundred per cent successful. Protracted misery makes millions desperate, and in an era of a global frontier-land and globalized crime one can hardly expect a shortage of 'businesses' eager to make a buck or a few billion bucks capitalizing on that desperation. Hence the second formidable consequence of the current transformation: millions of migrants wandering the routes once trodden by the 'surplus population' discharged by the greenhouses of modernity – only in a reverse direction, and this time unassisted (at any rate thus far) by the armies of *conquistadores*, tradesmen and missionaries. The full dimensions of that consequence and its repercussions are yet to unravel and to be grasped in all their many ramifications.

In a brief but sharp exchange of views that took place towards the end of 2001 in connection with the war on Afghanistan, Garry Younge mused on the condition of the planet a day *before* 11 September, that is before the day that by common agreement shook the world and ushered in a completely different phase of planetary history. He remembered 'a boatload of Afghan refugees floating off Australia' (to the applause of 90 per cent of Australians) to be in the end marooned on an uninhabited island in the middle of the Pacific Ocean:

> It is interesting now that they should have been Afghans, given that Australia is very involved in the coalition now, and thinks there is nothing better than a liberated Afghanistan and is prepared to send its bombs to liberate Afghanistan . . . Interesting also that we have now a Foreign Secretary who compares Afghanistan to the Nazis, but who, when he was Home Secretary and a group of Afghans landed at Stansted, said that there was no fear of persecution and sent them back.[13]

Younge concludes that on 10 September the world was 'a lawless place' in which the rich and the poor alike knew that 'might is right', that the high and mighty can ignore and bypass international law (or whatever is called by that name) whenever they find that law inconvenient, and that wealth and power determine not just economics but morality and the politics of global space and for that matter everything else concerning life conditions on the planet.

As I am writing, a case is being held in front of a High Court judge in London to test the legality of the treatment accorded to six asylum seekers, fleeing regimes officially recognized as 'evil' and/or as routinely violating, or negligent of, human rights, such as Iraq, Angola, Rwanda, Ethiopia and Iran.[14] Keir Starmer QC told the judge, Mr Justice Collins, that the new rules introduced in Britain have left hundreds of asylum seekers 'so destitute that they could not pursue their cases'. They were sleeping rough in the streets, were cold, hungry, scared and sick; some were 'reduced to living in telephone boxes and car parks'. They were allowed 'no funds, no accommodation and no food', and were prohibited from seeking paid work while being denied access to social benefits. And they had no control whatsoever over when, where and if their applications for asylum would be processed. A woman who had escaped from Rwanda after being repeatedly raped and beaten ended up spending the night on a chair at Croydon police station – on condition that she did not fall asleep. A man from Angola who found his father shot and his mother and sister left naked after a multiple rape ended up being denied all support and sleeping rough. Two hundred similar cases are currently waiting for the decision of the courts. In the case presented by Keir Starmer QC, the judge proclaimed the refusal of social assistance unlawful. The Home Secretary reacted to the verdict angrily: 'Frankly, I am personally fed up with having to deal with a situation where Parliament debates issues and the judges then overturn them . . . We don't accept what Mr Justice Collins has said. We will seek to overturn it.'[15]

The plight of the six whose case Keir Starmer QC presented is probably a side-effect of overcrowding and overflowing in the designed or improvised camps to which asylum seekers are routinely transported at the moment of landing. The numbers of homeless and stateless victims of globalization grow too fast for the designation and construction of camps to keep up.

One of the most sinister effects of globalization is the deregulation of wars. Most present-day warlike actions, and the most cruel and gory among them, are conducted by non-state entities, subject to no state laws and no international conventions. They are simultaneously outcomes and auxiliary but powerful causes of the continuous erosion of state sovereignty and the continuing frontier-land conditions in the 'interstate' global space. Intertribal antagonisms break into the open thanks to the weakening hands of the state, or in the case of the 'new states', of hands never given time to grow strong; once let loose, they render the inchoate or entrenched state-legislated laws unenforceable and practically null and void.

The population as a whole finds itself in a lawless space; the part of the population that decides to flee the battlefield and manages to escape finds itself in another type of lawlessness, that of the global frontier-land. Once outside the borders of their native country, escapees are deprived of the backing of a recognized state authority that could take them under its protection, vindicate their rights and intercede on their behalf with foreign powers. Refugees are stateless, but stateless in a new sense: their statelessness is raised to an entirely new level by the non-existence of a state authority to which their statehood could be referred. They are, as Michel Agier put it in his most insightful study of refugees in the era of globalization,[16] *hors du nomos* – *outside* law; not this or that law of this or that country, but *law as such*. They are outcasts and outlaws of a novel kind, the products of globalization and the fullest epitome and incarnation of its frontier-land spirit. To quote Agier again, they have been cast in a condition of 'liminal drift', with no way of knowing whether it is transitory or permanent. Even if they are stationary for a time, they are on a journey that is never completed since its destination (arrival or return) remains forever unclear, while a place they could call 'final' remains forever inaccessible. They are never to be free from the gnawing sense of the transience, indefiniteness and provisional nature of any settlement.

The plight of Palestinian refugees, many of whom have never experienced life outside the camps hastily patched together more than fifty years ago, has been well documented. As globalization takes its toll, though, new camps (less notorious and largely unnoticed or forgotten) mushroom around the spots of conflagration, prefiguring the model Tony Blair wishes the UN High Commission for Refugees to render obligatory. For instance, the three camps of Dabaab, populated by as many people as the rest of the Kenyan Garissa province in which they were located in 1991–2, show no signs of imminent closure, yet till this very day they do not appear on the map of the country. The same applies to the camps of Ilfo (opened in September 1991), Dagahaley (opened in March 1992) and Hagadera (opened in June 1992).[17]

On the way to the camps, their future inmates are stripped of every single element of their identities except one: that of stateless, placeless, functionless refugees. Inside the fences of the camp, they are pulped into a faceless mass, having been denied access to the elementary amenities from which identities are drawn and the usual yarns of which identities are woven. Becoming 'a refugee' means to lose

> the media on which social existence rests, that is a set of ordinary of things and persons that carry meanings – land, house, village, city, parents, possessions, jobs and other daily landmarks. These creatures in drift and waiting have nothing but their 'naked life', whose continuation depends on humanitarian assistance.[18]

As to the latter point, apprehensions abound. Is not the figure of a humanitarian assistant, whether hired or voluntary, itself an important link in the chain of exclusion? There are doubts whether the caring agencies doing their best to move people away from danger do not inadvertently assist the 'ethnic cleansers'. Agier muses whether the humanitarian worker is not an 'agent of exclusion at a lesser cost', and (more importantly still) a device designed to unload and dissipate the anxiety of the rest of the world, to absolve the guilty and placate the scruples, as well as defuse the sense of urgency and the fear of contingency. Putting the refugees in the hands of 'humanitarian workers' (and closing eyes to the armed guards in the background) seems to be the ideal way to reconcile the irreconcilable: the overwhelming wish to dispose of the noxious human waste while gratifying one's own poignant desire for moral righteousness.

> It may be that the guilty conscience caused by the plight of the damned part of humanity can be healed. To achieve that effect, it will suffice to allow the process of biosegregation, of conjuring up and fixing identities stained by wars, violence, exodus, diseases, misery and inequality – a process already in full swing – to take its course. The carriers of stigma would be definitely kept at a distance by reason of their lesser humanity, that is their physical as well as moral dehumanization.[19]

Refugees are human waste, with no useful function to play in the land of their arrival and temporary stay and no intention or realistic prospect of being assimilated and incorporated into the new social body; from their present place, the dumping site, there is no return and no road forward (unless it is a road towards yet more distant places, as in the case of the Afghan refugees escorted by Australian warships to an island far away from all beaten tracks). A distance large enough to prevent the poisonous effluvia of social decomposition from reaching places inhabited by their native inhabitants is the main criterion by which the location of their permanently temporary camps are selected. Out of that place, refugees are an obstacle and a trouble; inside that place, they are forgotten. In keeping them there and barring all leakage, in making the separation final and irreversible, 'compassion by some and hatred by others' cooperate in producing the same effect of taking distance and holding at a distance.[20]

Nothing is left but the walls, the barbed wire, the controlled gates, the armed guards. Between them they define the refugees' identity – or rather put paid to their right to self-definition. All waste, including wasted humans, tends to be piled up indiscriminately on the same refuse tip. The act of assigning to waste puts an end to differences, individualities, idiosyncrasies. Waste has no need of fine distinctions and subtle nuances, unless it is earmarked for recycling; but the refugees' prospects of being recycled into legitimate and acknowledged members of human society are, to say the least, dim and infinitely remote. All measures have been taken to assure the permanence of their exclusion. People without qualities have been deposited in a territory without denomination, whereas all the roads leading back to meaningful places and to the spots where socially legible meanings can be and are forged daily have been blocked for good.

The exact numbers of refugees scattered around the world is a matter of contention and likely to remain such, given that the very idea of 'refugee' – hiding as much as it reveals – is an 'essentially contested concept'. The most reliable figures available are produced bureaucratically, through registration and filing – primarily by the United Nations High Commissioner for Refugees (UNHCR) in the annual *The State of the World's Refugees* reports. The reports give the numbers of people already recognized as answering the UN definition of a 'refugee' and so of legitimate concern to the UNHCR. The latest report estimated the number of such people at 22.1 million (this figure does not include refugees under the care of other agencies, notably the 4 million

Palestinian refugees, and of course the persecuted minorities denied statehood who did not register anywhere or have been denied registration). Of the 22.1 million, 40 per cent were located by the end of 2000 in Asia, nearly 27 per cent in Europe, and slightly over 25 per cent in Africa. The most prolific suppliers of refugees were the territories of tribal conflicts and the target places of global military operations: Burundi, Sudan, Bosnia and Herzegovina, Iraq.[21] Most countries, UNHCR complains, 'do not subscribe to the definition' by which it operates. Even more countries insist on assurances that the temporary protection they are pressed to offer 'is indeed temporary' and that refugees will eventually be returned to their home countries or move elsewhere. 'Being under protection' does not mean 'being wanted' – and everything needed, and much more, is being done to prevent the refugees from confusing the two conditions.

Once a refugee, forever a refugee. Roads back to the lost (or rather no longer existing) homely paradise have been all but cut, and all exits from the purgatory of the camp lead to hell . . . The prospectless succession of empty days inside the perimeter of the camp may be tough to endure, but God forbid that the appointed or voluntary plenipotentiaries of humanity, whose job it is to keep the refugees inside the camp but away from perdition, pull the plug. But they do, time and again, whenever the powers-that-be decide that the exiles are no longer refugees since 'it is safe to return' to a homeland that has long ceased to be their homeland and has nothing to offer them that could be wished for. There are, for instance, about 900,000 refugees from the intertribal massacres and the battlefields of uncivil wars waged for decades in Ethiopia and Eritrea, scattered over the northern regions of Sudan, itself an impoverished, war-devastated country. They are mixed with other refugees who recall with horror the killing fields of southern Sudan.[22] By the decision of the UN agency endorsed by the non-governmental charities, they are no longer refugees and so are no longer entitled to humanitarian aid. They refused to go, however; apparently, they do not believe that there is 'a home' to which they could 'return', since the homes they remember have been either gutted or stolen. The new task of their humanitarian wardens is therefore to *make* them go . . . In Kassala camp, cutting of water supplies was followed by the forceful removal of inmates beyond the perimeter of the camp which just like their homes in Ethiopia has been razed to the ground to bar all thought of return. The same lot was visited on the inmates of Um Gulsam Laffa and Newshagarab camps. According to the local villagers' testimony, about 8,000 inmates perished when camp hospitals were closed, water wells dismantled and food delivery abandoned. It is difficult to verify their fate; though what one can be certain of is that hundreds of thousands have disappeared from the refugee registers and statistics even if they did not manage to escape from the nowhere-land of non-humanity.

Refugees, the human waste of the global frontier-land, are 'the outsiders incarnate', the absolute outsiders, outsiders everywhere and out of place everywhere except in places that are themselves out of place – the 'nowhere places' that appear on no maps used by ordinary humans on their travels. Once outside, indefinitely outside, a secure fence with watching towers is the only contraption needed to make the 'indefiniteness' of the out-of-place hold forever.

It is a different story with the redundant humans already 'inside' and bound to stay inside as the new fullness of the planet bars their territorial exclusion. In the absence of empty places to which they could be deported and the locking up of the places to which they would travel of their own free will in search of sustenance, waste-disposal sites must be laid out inside the locality which has made them supernumerary. Such sites emerge in all or most large cities. They are urban ghettoes; or rather, to follow Loïc Wacquant's insight, 'hyperghettoes'.[23]

Ghettoes, named or unnamed, are ancient institutions. They served the purpose of 'composite stratification' (and in one go 'multiple deprivation' as well), overlapping differentiation by caste or class with territorial separation. Ghettoes might be voluntary or involuntary (though only the latter tend to carry the stigma of the name), the main difference between the two being which side of the 'asymmetrical boundary' they faced – the obstacles piled up, respectively, at the entry to or at the exit from the ghetto territory.

Even in the case of 'involuntary ghettoes' there was, however, a modicum of 'pull' factors added to the decisive 'push' forces. They used to be 'mini societies', replicating in miniature all the major institutions that served the daily needs and life pursuits of those living outside the ghetto boundaries. They also provided its residents with a degree of security and at least a whiff of the feeling of *chez soi*, of being at home, unavailable to them outside. To quote Wacquant's description of the pattern dominant in the black American ghettoes of the last century:

> the black bourgeoisie's [doctors, lawyers, teachers, businessmen] economic power rested on supplying goods and services to its lower-class brethren; and all 'brown' residents of the city were united in their common rejection of caste subordination and abiding concern to 'advance the race' . . . As a result, the postwar ghetto was *integrated both socially and structurally* – even the 'shadies' who earned their living from such illicit trades as the 'numbers game', liquor sale, prostitution and other *risqué* recreations, were entwined with the different classes.[24]

The orthodox ghettoes might have been enclosures surrounded by insurmountable, even if non-material, barriers (physical and social) and with the few remaining exits exceedingly difficult to negotiate. They might have been instruments of class-and-caste segregation and might have branded their residents with the stigma of inferiority and social rejection. Unlike the 'hyperghettoes' that have grown out of them and took their place towards the end of the last century, they were not however dumping sites for the surplus, redundant, unemployable and functionless population. Unlike its classical predecessor, the new ghetto, in Wacquant's words, 'serves not as a reservoir of disposable industrial labour but a mere dumping ground [for those for whom] the surrounding society has no economic or political use'. Abandoned by their own middle classes, who ceased to rely on black clientele alone and chose to buy their way into the higher grade security of the voluntary ghettoes of 'gated communities', the ghetto dwellers cannot create on their own substitute economic or political uses to replace the uses denied to them by the greater society. As a result, 'whereas the ghetto in its classical form acted partly

as a protective shield against brutal racial exclusion, the hyper-
ghetto has lost its positive role of collective buffer, making it a
deadly machinery for naked social relegation.'

In other words: the American black ghetto has turned purely
and simply into a, virtually single-purpose, waste disposal tip. 'It
has devolved into a one-dimensional machinery for naked relegation, a human warehouse wherein are discarded those segments
of urban society deemed disreputable, derelict, and dangerous.'

Wacquant notices and lists a number of parallel and mutually
coordinated processes that bring the American black ghettoes ever
closer to the model of prisonlike Goffmanesque 'total institutions': a 'prisonization' of public housing ever more reminiscent
of houses of detention, with new 'projects' 'fenced up, their
perimeter placed under beefed-up security patrols and authori-
tarian controls' – and as Jerome G. Miller noted, 'random searches,
segregation, curfews, and resident counts – all familiar procedures
of efficient prison management';[25] and the transformation of
state-maintained schools into 'institutions of confinement' whose
primary mission is not to educate but to ensure 'custody and
control' – 'Indeed, it appears that that the main purpose of these
schools is simply to "neutralize" youth considered unworthy and
unruly by holding them under lock for the day so that, at
minimum, they do not engage in street crime.'

There is a movement in the opposite direction, transforming
the nature of American prisons, their manifest and latent functions, their declared and tacit purposes and their physical structures and routines, so that urban ghettoes and prisons meet
halfway, their meeting place being the explicit role of a dumping
ground for human waste. To quote Wacquant again, 'The "Big
House" that embodied the correctional ideal of melioristic treatment and community reintegration of inmates gave way to a
race-divided and violence-ridden "warehouse" geared solely to
neutralizing social rejects by sequestering them physically from
society.'[26]

As far as other urban ghettoes are concerned, and particularly
the ghettoes emerging in the great number of European cities with
a significant immigrant population, a similar transformation may
be fairly advanced but remains incomplete. Racially or ethnically

pure urban ghettoes remain a rarity in Europe. Besides, unlike the American blacks, the recent and relatively recent immigrants who populate them are not locally produced human waste; they are 'imported waste' from other countries with a lingering hope of recycling. The question of whether such 'recycling' is or is not on the cards and so whether the verdict of assignment to waste is final and globally binding remains open. These urban ghettoes remain, we may say, 'halfway inns' or 'two-way streets'. It is because of that provisional, undecided, underdefined character that they are the sources and the target of acute tension erupting daily into reconnaissance skirmishes and boundary clashes.

This ambiguity that sets the immigrant and thus far mixed-population ghettoes of European towns apart from the American 'hyperghettoes' may not however last. As Philippe Robert found, French urban ghettoes that originally had the character of 'transit' or 'passage' stations for new immigrants who were expected soon to be assimilated and ingested by established urban structures turned into 'spaces of relegation' once employment was deregu-lated, becoming precarious and volatile, and unemployment became durable. It was then that the resentment and animosity of the established population grew into a virtually impenetrable wall locking out the newcomers-turned-outsiders. The *quartiers*, already socially degraded and cut off from communication with other parts of the cities, were now 'the only places where [the immigrants] could feel *chez soi*, sheltered from the malevolent looks of the rest of the population'.[27]

Hughes Lagrange and Thierry Pech note in addition that once the state, having abandoned most of its economic and social func-tions, selected a 'policy of security' (and more concretely of per-sonal safety) as the hub of its strategy aimed at recouping its fallen authority and the restoration of its protective importance in the eyes of the citizenry, the influx of newcomers was overtly or obliquely blamed for the rising uneasiness and diffuse fears ema-nating from the ever more precarious labour market.[28] The immi-grants' *quartiers* were depicted as hothouses of petty criminality, begging and prostitution, which were accused in their turn of playing a major role in the rising anxiety of 'ordinary citizens'. To the acclaim of its citizens desperately seeking the roots of their incapacitating anxiety, the state flexed its muscle, however flabby and indolent in all other domains, in full public view – criminal-izing those margins of the population who were the most feeble and living the most precariously, designing ever more stringent and severe 'firm hand' policies and waging spectacular anti-crime campaigns focused on the human waste of foreign origin dumped in the suburbs of French cities.

Loïc Wacquant notes a paradox:

> The same people who yesterday fought with visible success for 'less state' to set free capital and the way it used the labour force, ardu-ously demand today 'more state' to contain and hide the dele-terious social consequences of the deregulation of employment conditions and the deterioration of social protection for the inferior regions of social space.[29]

Of course, what Wacquant noted is anything but a paradox. The apparent change of heart strictly follows the logic of the passage from the recycling to the disposal of human waste. The passage was radical enough to need the keen and energetic assistance of state power, and the state obliged.

It did it first by dismantling collective forms of insurance to cover individuals who fell off the productive treadmill (tem-porarily, it was assumed). It was the kind of insurance that made obvious sense to both left and right wings of the political spec-trum as long as the fall (and thus the assignment to productive waste) was deemed to be a temporary mishap, ushering in a brief stage of recycling ('rehabilitating', then returning to active service in the industrial force). But it quickly lost its 'beyond left and right' support once the prospects of recycling started to look remote and uncertain and the facilities of regular recycling looked increasingly incapable of accommodating all who had fallen or who had never risen in the first place.

Second, the state obliged by designing and building new secure waste-disposal sites – an endeavour certain to command ever growing popular support as the hopes of successful recycling faded, as the traditional method of human-waste disposal (through the exportation of surplus labour) ceased to be available, and as the suspicion of human universal disposability deepened and spread wider, together with the horror that the sight of 'wasted humans' evoked.

The social state is gradually, yet relentlessly and consistently, turned into a 'garrison state', as Henry A.Giroux calls it, describing it as a state that increasingly protects the interests of global, transnational corporations 'while stepping up the level of repression and militarization on the domestic front'. Social problems are increasingly criminalized. In Giroux's summary,

> Repression increases and replaces compassion. Real issues such as a tight housing market and massive unemployment in the cities – as causes of homelessness, youth loitering and drug epidemics – are overlooked in favour of policies associated with discipline, containment and control.[30]

The immediate proximity of large and growing agglomerations of 'wasted humans', likely to become durable or permanent, calls for stricter segregationist policies and extraordinary security measures, lest the 'health of society', the 'normal functioning' of the social system, be endangered. The notorious tasks of 'tension management' and 'pattern maintenance' that, according to Talcott Parsons, each system needs to perform in order to survive presently boil down almost entirely to the tight separation of 'human waste' from the rest of society, its exemption from the legal framework in which the life pursuits of the rest of society are conducted, and its 'neutralization'. 'Human waste' can no longer be removed to distant waste disposal sites and placed firmly out of bounds to 'normal life'. It needs therefore to be sealed off in tightly closed containers.

The penal system supplies such containers. In David Garland's succinct and precise summary of the current transformation, prisons which in the era of recycling 'functioned as the deep end of the correctional sector' are today 'conceived much more explicitly as a mechanism of exclusion and control'. It is the walls, and not what happens inside the walls, that 'are now seen as the institution's most important and valuable element'.[31] At best, the

intention to 'rehabilitate', to 'reform', to 're-educate' and to return
the stray sheep to the flock is only paid an occasional lip service
– and when it is, it is countered with an angry chorus baying for
blood, with the leading tabloids in the role of conductors and
leading politicians singing all the solo parts. Explicitly, the main
and perhaps the sole purpose of prisons is not just any human-
waste disposal but a final, definitive disposal. Once rejected,
forever rejected. For a former prisoner on parole or on probation,
a return to society is almost impossible and a return to prison
almost certain. Instead of guiding and easing the road 'back to the
community' for prisoners who have served their term of punishment, the function of probation officers is keeping the community safe from the perpetual danger temporarily let loose. 'The
interests of convicted offenders, insofar as they are considered at
all, are viewed as fundamentally opposed to those of the public.'[32]

Indeed, offenders tend to be viewed as 'intrinsically evil
and wicked', they 'are not like us'. All similarities are purely
accidental . . .

> There can be no mutual intelligibility, no bridge of understanding,
> no real communication between 'us' and 'them' . . .
>   Whether the offender's character is the result of bad genes or
> of being reared in an anti-social culture, the outcome is the same
> – a person who is beyond the pale, beyond reform, outside the civil
> community . . .
>   Those who do not or cannot fit in must be excommunicated and
> forcibly expelled.[33]

In a nutshell, prisons, like so many other social institutions, have
moved from the task of recycling to that of waste disposal. They
have been reallocated to the front line of the battle to resolve the
crisis in which the waste disposal industry has fallen as a result
of the global triumph of modernity and the new fullness of the
planet. All waste is potentially poisonous – or at least, being
defined as waste, it is deemed to be contaminating and disturbing
to the proper order of things. If recycling is no longer profitable
and its chances (at any rate in the present-day setting) are no
longer realistic, the right way to deal with waste is to speed up its

'biodegradation' and decomposition while isolating it as securely as possible from the ordinary human habitat.

> Work, social welfare, and family support used to be the means whereby ex-prisoners were reintegrated into mainstream society. With the decline of these resources, imprisonment has become a longer-term assignment from which individuals have little prospect of returning to an unsupervised freedom . . .
> The prison is used today as a kind of reservation, a quarantine zone in which purportedly dangerous individuals are segregated in the name of public safety.[34]

Building more prisons, making more offences punishable by imprisonment, the policy of 'zero tolerance' and harsher and longer sentences are best understood as so many efforts to rebuild the failing and faltering waste disposal industry – on a new foundation more in keeping with the novel conditions of the globalized world.

There is also another kind of waste directly linked to the globalization process in its present form: a kind of waste whose origins can be traced back to globalization's 'frontier-land' conditions and one that globalization in such a form cannot but turn out daily in Manuel Castells's 'space of flows'.

As has been already suggested, under classical 'frontier-land' conditions cattle barons and outlaws were in tacit agreement: neither of them wished the lawlessness and the rule of the quickest and the shrewdest and the least scrupulous to grind to a halt and be replaced with the government of law. They both thrived on the absence of routine, on fluidity of alliances and front lines and on the overall frailty of commitments, rights and obligations. Such a convergence of interests did not augur well for the personal safety of everyone inside the frontier-land, whatever precautions residents or travellers took to insure themselves against the danger. It made the frontier-land a site of perpetual uncertainty and at the same time made insecurity immune to all effective intervention. Insecurity could not be confronted at its source; like the coalitions and the battlefields, the resulting anxiety was free-floating, unsure of its targets and selecting them at random. Frontier-land conditions are best conveyed by Jurij Lotman's metaphor of the minefield, of which one can say with a high degree of certainty that explosions will occur there, but can only guess at their timing and location.

In the present-day rendition of frontier-land conditions the place of cattle barons has been taken by global manufacturing, trade and capital companies, while the free-roaming bandits, single or in gangs, have been replaced by terrorist networks and an indefinable number of scattered individuals who spy in terrorist acts an archetype for their own private battles with individually suffered traumas or simply a hint as to how even a snubbed and spurned wretch can go down with a bang.

The acts of both major adversaries/partners in the frontier-land game add profusely to the production of human waste. The first are most active in the 'economic progress' branch of the industry, the second in the 'creative destruction of order' branch – a thoroughly deregulated version of the coercive undertakings in which modern states used to be engrossed from the start even while claiming monopoly on designing and building social order.

No authority can claim today an exclusive grip over its ostensibly sovereign territory. Even the most closely guarded borders are porous and prove easy to penetrate; courtesy of shock-greedy media, the massive forces summoned to protect borderlines against leaks and break-ins (like the widely publicized sight of tanks at Heathrow) daily remind the public of the ultimate vanity of the effort. Strikingly different and often incompatible ideas of the right and proper order of things meet and clash inside each ostensibly sovereign territory, their champions and foot soldiers vying with each other to lift the world to the height of their idea – though invariably at the expense of the residents, transformed in the process into thoroughly disposable props of the battle scene, the 'collateral damage' of the actions of war.

In the era of globalization, the 'collateral damage' and 'collateral casualties' left behind by the continuously sizzling and occasionally erupting enmities between the liquid modern versions of cattle barons and mounted bandits turn gradually into the staple and most voluminous products of the waste industry. While (in theory at least, if not in practice) one can fight tooth and nail against an adverse verdict delivered by the authority in judgement, fight to reverse the verdict, argue to prove one's case, appeal to a higher court in case your argument is rejected, try to arouse public indignation and protest, and if all that fails seek rescue in an escape from the realm of the court's sovereignty – none of such expedients are available to the victims of 'collateral damage'. There is no authority they may resist, sue, lay charges against, or demand compensation from. They are the waste of the ongoing creative destruction of global legal, political and ethical order.

Under such circumstances no line drawn to separate 'the waste' from a 'useful product' is likely to remain uncontested and no sentence condemning to a life-on-a-refuse-heap is likely to hold for long without an opposition trying hard to overthrow and reverse it. And so no one feels truly secure amidst the uncounted number of competing design-and-build projects. No one can rely on a recent or currently enforced verdict, however powerful the authority that delivered it might be. No one can assume that the spectre of a disposal tip has been once and for all exorcised and the danger of being rejected and consigned to waste definitely averted. The overall impression is one of randomness, unalloyed contingency, blind fate – and against haphazard sequences, unaccountable accidents and *non sequiturs*, just as against ad hoc alliances of powers held together or dismantled by bribery or blackmail, there is no conceivable defence. One can possibly avoid being a victim, but nothing can be done to escape the fate of being a 'collateral casualty'. That adds a wholly new sinister dimension to the spectre of uncertainty that hovers above the world remade into a global frontier-land.

The 'social state', that crowning of the long history of European democracy and until recently its dominant form, is today in retreat. The social state based its legitimacy and rested its demands for the loyalty and obedience of its citizens on the promise to defend them and insure against redundancy, exclusion and rejection as well as against random blows of fate – against being consigned to 'human waste' because of individual inadequacies or misfortunes; in short, on the promise to insert certainty and

security into lives in which chaos and contingency would otherwise rule. If hapless individuals stumbled and fell, there would be
someone around ready to hold their hands and help them to their
feet again.

Erratic conditions of employment buffeted by market competition were then, as they continue to be, the major source of the
uncertainty about the future and the insecurity of social standing
and self-esteem that haunted the citizens. It was primarily against
that uncertainty that the *social* state undertook to protect its subjects – by making jobs more secure and the future more assured.
For the reasons already discussed this is however no longer the
case. The contemporary state cannot deliver on the social state's
promise and its politicians no longer repeat the promise. Instead,
their policies portend a yet more precarious, risk-ridden life calling
for a lot of brinkmanship while making life projects all but impossible; they call on the electors to be 'more flexible' (that is, to
brace themselves for yet more insecurity to come) and to seek
individually their own individual solutions to the socially produced troubles.

A most urgent imperative faced by every government presiding over the dismantling and demise of the social state is therefore the task of finding or construing a new 'legitimation formula'
on which the self-assertion of state authority and the demand of
discipline may rest instead. Being felled as a 'collateral casualty'
of economic progress, now in the hands of free-floating global economic forces, is not a plight which state governments can credi-
bly promise to stave off. But beefing up fears about the threat to
personal safety from similarly free-floating terrorist conspirators,
and then promising more security guards, a denser net of X-ray
machines and a wider scope for closed-circuit television, more
frequent checks and more pre-empting strikes and precautionary
arrests to protect that safety, looks like an expedient alternative.

By contrast with the all-too-tangible and daily experienced
insecurity manufactured by the markets, which need no help
from political powers except to be left alone, the mentality of a
'besieged fortress' and of individual bodies and private possessions
under threat must be actively cultivated. Threats must be painted
in the most sinister of colours, so that the *non-materialization of*

threats rather than the advent of the foreboded apocalypse can be presented to the frightened public as an *extraordinary* event, and above all as the result of the exceptional skills, vigilance, care and goodwill of state organs. And this is done, and to spectacular effect. Almost daily, and at least once a week, the CIA and the FBI warn Americans of imminent attempts on their safety, casting them into a state of constant security alert and holding them there, putting individual safety firmly into the focus of the most varied and diffuse tensions – while the American President keeps reminding his electors that 'it would take one vial, one canister, one crate slipped into this country to bring a day of horror like none we have ever known.' That strategy is eagerly, even if so far with somewhat less ardour (less because of lack of funds rather than will), copied by other governments overseeing the burial of the social state. A new popular demand for a strong state power capable of resuscitating the fading hopes of protection against a confinement to waste is built on the foundation of *personal* vulnerability and *personal* safety, instead of *social* precariousness and *social* protection.

As in so many other cases, so also in the development of that new legitimation formula America plays a pioneering, pattern-setting role. There is little wonder that many a government facing the same task looks towards America with sympathetic anticipation, finding in its policies a useful example to follow. Underneath the ostensible and openly aired differences of opinion on the ways to proceed there seems to be a genuine 'union of minds' between the governments, not at all reducible to the momentary coincidence of transient interests; an unwritten, tacit agreement of state power holders on a common legitimation policy. That this may be the case is shown in the zeal with which the British Prime Minister, watched with rising interest by other European prime ministers, embraces and imports all American novelties related to the production of a 'state of emergency' – such as locking up the 'aliens' (euphemistically called 'asylum seekers') in camps, giving 'security considerations' unquestioned priority over human rights, writing off or suspending many a human right that has stayed in force since the time of the Magna Carta and habeas corpus, a 'zero tolerance' policy towards alleged 'budding criminals', and

regularly repeated warnings that *some*where, *some*time, *some* terrorists will most surely strike. We are all potential candidates for
the role of 'collateral casualties' in a war we did not declare and
to which we did not give our consent. When measured against
that threat, hammered home as much more immediate and dra-
matic, it is hoped that the orthodox fears of social redundancy will
be dwarfed and possibly even put to sleep.

'Collateral damage' was a term that might have been specifically invented to denote the human waste specific to the new
planetary frontier-land conditions created by the impetuous and
unrestrained globalization drive that thus far effectively resists all
attempts at taming and regulating it. Fears related to that variety
of modern waste production seem to overshadow the more traditional waste related apprehensions and anxieties. Little wonder
that they are most eagerly employed in the construction (and so
also in the attempts at deconstruction) of new planet-wide power
hierarchies.

These new kinds of fear also dissolve trust, the binding agent of
all human togetherness. Epicurus, the ancient sage, already noted
(in the letter to Menoeceus) that 'it is not so much our friends'
help that helps us as the confident knowledge that they will help
us.' Without trust, the web of human commitments falls apart,
making the world a yet more dangerous and fearsome place. The
fears aroused by the frontier-land variety of waste tend to be self-
reproducing, self-corroborating and self-magnifying.

Trust is replaced by universal suspicion. All bonds are assumed
to be untrustworthy, unreliable, trap-and-ambush-like – until
proven otherwise; but in the absence of trust the very idea of a
'proof', let alone a clinching and final proof, is anything but clear
and convincing. What would a credible, really trustworthy proof
be like? You wouldn't recognize it if you saw it; even staring it in
the face, you wouldn't believe that it was indeed what it was pre-
tending to be. The acceptance of proof, therefore, needs to be post-
poned indefinitely. The efforts at tying up and fastening bonds line
up in an infinite sequence of experiments. Being experimental,
accepted 'on a trial basis' and perpetually on trial, always of a provisional 'let's wait and see how they work' kind, human alliances,

commitments and bonds are unlikely to solidify enough to be proclaimed fully and truly reliable. Born of suspicion, they beget suspicion.

Commitments (employment contracts, wedding agreements, 'living together' arrangements) are entered into with a 'cancellation option' in mind; and by the firmness of the 'opt out' clauses is their quality judged and desirability measured. In other words, it is clear from the very start that a waste disposal site will indeed be, as it should and as it is bound to be, their ultimate destination. From the moment of their birth, commitments are seen and treated as prospective waste. Frailty (of the biodegradable sort) is therefore seen as their advantage. It is easy to forget that the bond-tying commitments were sought in the first place, and continue to be sought, for the sake of putting paid to that mind-boggling and blood-curdling fragility of human existence . . .

Bereaved of trust, saturated with suspicion, life is shot through with antinomies and ambiguities it cannot resolve. Hoping to get on under the sign of waste, it stumbles from a disappointment to a frustration, each time landing at the very point it wished to escape when starting its journey of exploration. A life so lived leaves behind a string of faulty and abandoned relationships – the waste of the global frontier-land conditions notorious for recasting trust as a sign of naivety and as a trap for the unresourceful and gullible.

4

Culture of waste

In the convoluted history of the production and disposal of human waste, the vision of 'eternity' and its present fall from grace have played a crucial role.

Only infinity is fully and truly all-inclusive. Infinity and exclusion are incompatible; and so are infinity and exemption. In the infinity of time and space everything may happen, and everything must happen. Everything that was, is and yet may come into being has its place. It is only the idea of 'no room' that has no room in infinity. The idea that infinity absolutely cannot accommodate is that of redundancy – of waste.

This is what Joseph Cartaphilus of Smyrna, the hero of a Jorge Luis Borges story, *The Immortal*, found out in the City of the Immortals:

> Taught by centuries of living, the republic of immortal men had achieved a perfection of tolerance, almost of disdain. They knew that over an infinitely long span of time, all things happen to all men. As reward for his past and future virtues, every man merited every kindness ... The most fleeting thought obeys an invisible plan, and may crown, or inaugurate, a secret design ... No one is someone; a single immortal man is all men.[1]

In infinity nothing can be devoid of meaning, even if that meaning appears illegible and inscrutable to human beings, who due to their limited lifespan have no access to the kind of time needed to decipher it or to witness its revelation. In infinity, everything is *recycled no end* as in the Hindu idea of eternal return and reincarnation, or *forever existing* as in the Christian idea of a linear progress from the earthly habitat of mortal flesh to the netherworld of souls where the true meaning of human deeds is fathomed, judged, and rewarded or punished accordingly. In infinity, individual humans may disappear from the view of mortals, but no one sinks irreversibly into nothingness, and every judgement, except the last one, infinitely remote, is premature and a testimony of fraud or sinful conceit if it is claimed to be final.

'Infinity' is of course but an abstract construct, a mental extrapolation from the experience of the long term; an extrapolation prompted by the incapacitating brevity of bodily life and the vexing incompleteness of life's labours. The idea of infinity stands for an imagined extension of the present in which the sense of all past, current and future moments will be revealed and everything will fall into place; all labours will bear their benign or poisonous fruits, merits will be rewarded and vices punished – or, rather, deeds will be classified as merits or vices depending on their as yet unknown aftermath, that is, on their far-reaching, genuinely ultimate consequences. It is because the consequences are not open to experience and cannot be known in full when the chain of events is set in motion that whatever happens, matters – *must* matter. In infinity, there is nothing that happens of which you may say that it is redundant, attached to the flow of events by sheer accident, not really necessary, disposable; that it does not fit into the (incomprehensible to you) scheme of things and does not count in the (impenetrable to you) fullness of time. Whatever was, must have been a part of God's design and the Divine Chain of Being, and it was beyond human power to pass verdicts on the propriety and wisdom of its presence; the most humans could do was to struggle to penetrate its hidden purpose. In God's Design nothing can be redundant – even if the feeble human mind thinks it to be so and the sinful nature of humans prompts them to behave as if it were. In the Divine Chain of Being, nothing is redundant, whatever humans may do to make it so.

It is for that reason that – as Hans Jonas pithily put it – we 'number our days and make them count'.[2] Paradoxically, it is not so much the eternal duration itself, but the coupling of immortality with the mortality of individual humans, with the brevity of individual existence, that impregnates each day with meaning. 'As to each of us, the knowledge that we are here but briefly and a nonnegotiable limit is set to our expected time may even be necessary as the incentive to number our days and make them count' – to imbue with lasting significance whatever we do and to search for a deeper meaning in everything that happens.

The humbling and painful clash between the severely limited individual presence on earth and the unperturbed solidity of the world has been an integral part of human experience since the beginning of history. Until the dawn of modernity, life was a daily confrontation between the transience of the first and the duration of the second, and a daily rehearsal of the irreparable incommensurability between the two. In the bid for duration, all odds were on the side of the world, bound to outlive every human individual currently alive.

As long as this state of affairs lasted, the idea of infinity was secure, and so was its legislative and executive, meaning-bestowing power over human earthly life. Their security began to be eroded once humans set out to 'melt all that is solid' and to 'profane everything sacred' (which, by this account, are but two ways of expressing the same attitude and the same action). That security crumbled once, in the 'liquid' phase of the modern era, the odds in the game of survival moved from the world 'out there' to the individual life – currently an entity with a life expectation *longer* than that of any element of its life setting and the sole entity with a *rising* longevity of life expectation.

If the premodern life was a daily rehearsal of the infinite duration of everything except mortal life, the liquid modern life is a daily rehearsal of universal transience. Nothing in the world is bound to last, let alone last forever. Today's useful and indispensable objects, with but few exceptions, are tomorrow's waste. Nothing is truly necessary, nothing is irreplaceable. Everything is born with a branding of imminent death; everything leaves the production line with a 'use-by date' label attached; constructions do not start unless permissions to demolish (if required) have been issued, and contracts are not signed unless their duration is fixed or their termination allowed depending on the hazards of the future. No step and no choice is once and for all, none is irrevocable. No commitment lasts long enough to reach the point of no return. All things, born or made, human or not, are until-further-notice and dispensable. A spectre hovers over the denizens of the liquid modern world and all their labours and creations: the spectre of redundancy.

Liquid modernity is a civilization of excess, redundancy, waste and waste disposal.

Excursus: *Culture and eternity* We, the humans, know that we are mortal – bound to die. This knowledge is difficult to live with. Living with such knowledge would be downright impossible were it not for culture. Culture, the great human invention (perhaps the greatest of them all; a meta-invention, an invention setting inventiveness in motion and making all other inventions possible), is a contraption to render the human kind of living, the kind of living that entails knowledge of mortality, bearable – in defiance of logic and reason.

By all conceivable standards, this is not a mean achievement in itself. But culture does more than that: it manages somehow to *recast the horror of death into a moving force of life*. It kneads the *meaningfulness* of life out of death's *absurdity*. 'Society everywhere', as Ernest Becker points out, 'is a living myth of the significance of human life, a defiant creation of meaning.'[3] At least this is what 'societies everywhere' used to do, though the way of doing it varied from one place to another and from one era to another, with strikingly different impacts on the form and style of human life.

What all such forms and styles had in common was the authoring and authorization of some recipe for the transcendence of mortality. This is in fact what Becker has in mind when he suggests that 'society is a codified hero system'; that it is designed to serve as 'a vehicle for earthly heroism' meant to induce 'the hope and belief' . . . 'that the things that man creates in society are of lasting worth and meaning, that they outlive and outshine death and decay, that man and his products count'.[4]

Let me comment, though, right away that the term 'heroism' may mislead. Accepting the recipe on offer, swallowing the recommended dose of the prescribed drug, and altogether keeping in line and following faithfully the routines promised to lead from here to eternity, require neither the kind of courage nor the readiness for self-sacrifice that we tend to associate with the idea of heroic acts. At best, the bustle to outshine death with the help of implements for whose power to outshine death society has vouched is an artful magic on a par with the alchemists' feat: securing duration, perhaps an eternal duration, while deploying sorely fragile raw material and evidently transient powers. It is, no doubt, an outstanding, extraordinary, mind-boggling accomplishment of a magnitude that may retrospectively justify the claim to the title of hero. That title however makes sense only as a privilege offered to a chosen few, while the point about society being a 'hero *system*' is, on the contrary, that the ways and means to such an accomplishment are put at the disposal of ordinary people who lack the exquisite, rare talents and valour of the admittedly tiny bunch of gallant warriors for whom the idea of 'heroism' in its original sense was designed. The stratagem would not work, society could hardly become a 'hero *system*', unless '*everybody* could do it'. To put it bluntly, the phrase 'hero system' is an oxymoron.

Even if different kinds of people are offered different vehicles intended to transport them into eternity, the most crucial division between such vehicles is, one may say, the difference between private cars and public buses. Becker's suggestion needs a correction. *Society, and the culture that makes human society into a system, is a contraption that allows the heroic feat to be accomplished, daily and matter-of-factly, by non-heroic, ordinary human beings.*

There are, in fact, two stratagems of culture that make living with the knowledge of the inevitability of death bearable – not one.

The most common stratagem does not require any kind of heroism, whether narrowly or widely understood. As a matter of fact, the function of that stratagem is to abolish, or at least suspend, the very need to be heroic – through leaving little room for the kinds of situations that may force the issue of transcendence on to life's agenda. As Blaise Pascal long ago observed, 'Being unable to cure death . . . men have decided, in order to be happy', 'not to think about such things'. Indeed, Pascal adds, 'it is easier to bear death when one is not thinking about it than the idea of death when there is no danger' – the implication being that real dangers take hold of the mind, drain the emotions and exhaust every bit of energy for action, so that in the moment of danger one is less likely to muse on death than one does at leisure.

Other pastimes, less testing and risky than fighting off mortal threats, though no less absorbing, are socially practised with a very similar effect: squeezing meditation on death out of daily life pursuits. These are, in Pascal's opinion, *diversions*, which fill the available time from beginning to end, with no empty and idle moment left in which to allow thoughts to wander aimlessly, lest they may focus by chance on the ultimate vanity of the allegedly important and engrossing, because time-and-energy consuming, life concerns. 'What people want is not the easy peaceful life that allows us to think of our unhappy condition', 'but the agitation that takes our mind off it and diverts us'.[5] This preference makes us put the hunt above the capture: 'The hare itself would not save us from thinking about death . . . but hunting it does so' (or, as Robert Louis Stevenson's adage had it, to travel hopefully is better than to arrive). A dead hare might be at the bottom of the hunter's list of priorities, but the hunting is at the top of that list, and must stay there, since however vain it might be itself, its vanity is indispensable to cover up that other vanity that truly counts.

Max Scheler noted the consequences of the wide application of the 'diversion stratagem'. Unlike Pascal, however, Scheler saw escape through diversion as an event in history rather than a perpetual human predicament: an outcome of the modern revolution in the mode of being. He deplored that novelty as a mortal danger to the human urge of transcendence.

Death has been removed out of the sight of contemporary men and women, it 'is no longer visible'. That 'non-being of death' has become, in Scheler's opinion, the 'negative illusion of the modern type of consciousness'.[6] No longer a part of human destiny that needs to be faced up to in all its majesty and duly respected, death has been demoted to the status of a deplorable catastrophe, like a pistol shot or a brick falling from a roof. With the horizon of mortality effectively removed from its vision and no longer orienting long-term projects or ordering daily pursuits, life has lost its inner cohesion. Life is lived from one day to the next 'until by a curious coincidence there is no next day'. But once the *fear of death* had receded or vanished from daily life, it failed to bring in its wake the hoped-for spiritual quiescence. It was promptly replaced by the *fear of life*. That other fear, in its turn, prompts a 'calculating approach to life' that feeds on an unquenchable thirst for ever new possessions and the cult of 'progress' – by itself a meaningless idea,

devoid of purpose. 'Making progress', here Scheler quotes Werner
Sombart's memorable verdict, is its only practical sense.

The relentless devaluation of the 'long term' as such is a common
denominator of the qualities already lost or ominously thin on the
ground and threatened with extinction: the qualities of things and
states that are solid, durable and lasting, and ultimately of *eternity*, of which all those phenomena were but imperfect, though
wistful and hopeful, approximations . . . Eternity, one is tempted to
conclude, has had its day; a very long day it was, as a matter of fact
– lasting many years, centuries and millennia. Eternity had seemed
to be a trustworthy human companion/guide since the beginning
of humanity. It seems, though, that the ways of eternity and
humanity have parted or are about to part; men and women need
now to walk the road from childhood to senility with no inkling of
the sense of their travel and no confidence in the meaningfulness
of it all.

Eternity has been one of culture's few genuine universals. To the
sober, logically trained mind this may seem strange, at first glance
at least; indeed, it takes a lot of imagination even to *conceive of*
'eternal duration', while *visualizing* it defies the power of human
senses. In no form can 'eternity' be gleaned from the 'inside' of
human experience. It cannot be seen, touched, heard, sniffed or
savoured. And yet one would search in vain for a human population that did not consider eternity anything but self-evident.
Awareness of eternity (should we rather say, belief in eternity) can
indeed be taken as one of the defining traits of humanity.

The resolution of that paradox seems to lie in another human
universal: language. Or, rather in another paradox, inextricably
linked to the possession of language.

Because we, human beings, have language, we cannot but be
aware that all living creatures are mortal, and so too each one of
us; we (more to the point: *I*) will die, as sooner or later will all other
humans we know or know of, all those men and women with
whose lives our lives are intertwined. Yet by the same reason none
of us is tied to the immediate reality of experience. Language may
inform us how *things* are, but language is also a knife that cuts us,
the word-makers, word-users and words' creatures, free from
things as they are and from the immediacy of their presence. Using
words as yarn, we can weave canvases that do not picture any
'reality' that we (or for that matter any other language users)
have experienced. The veracity and trustworthiness of such 'non-

representational' canvases do not differ markedly from those of the rest. And so, courtesy of language, we can 'experience' by proxy a world from which we, whose world it is, have been removed: a world that *does not contain us, the world as it might be* when *we are no more*. Such a world is frightening; it dwarfs and denigrates whatever we do or may do while we are still part of it. The no-leave-to-appeal refusal of admission to that world is the most painful of all humiliating, dignity-denying rejections; perhaps even the archetype that turns rejection, blackballing, blacklisting, snubbing, banishing and ostracizing, its pale copies, into the acts of supreme cruelty that they are.

In the pharmacy of language, though, the poison jars tend to come complete with an admixture of the antidote. In the presently pondered case, the pain of transience comes together with the intimation of perpetual duration. Finitude is wrapped in one parcel with infinity, brevity with eternity, mortality with life after death.

As George Steiner puts it,

> It is because we can tell stories, fictive or mathematical-cosmological, about a universe a billion years hence; it is because we can ... conceptualise the Monday morning after our cremation; it is because 'if' sentences ... can, spoken at will, deny, reconstruct, alter past, present and future, mapping *otherwise* the determinants of pragmatic reality, that existence continues to be worth experiencing. Hope is grammar.[7]

This feat, Steiner hastens to add, is nothing short of a miracle. Just think of 'the future of "to be", of the "shall" and the "will", whose articulations generate the breathing-spaces of fear and of hope, of renewal and innovation which are the cartography of the unknown'. The amazement felt at the stupendous, awe-inspiring accomplishment of human inventiveness is itself hardly amazing; the package deal is truly astounding. Purchasing vanity in a package deal with worthiness, the absurd with sense, fear with hope, has been perhaps the best bargain humanity ever struck.

The invention of eternity is indeed the magic of language; it is a curious and remarkable invention – and yet an inevitable one, something that could not *not* be invented. Really inconceivable would be a human-like, linguistically endowed species that failed to invent eternity – and it would be inconceivable for the sheer reason of being able to remain unaware of its own mortality. On its own, however, in its pristine, raw, unprocessed form, the vision of eternity would only have added to the despair sown by the certainty of death. In order to wrap fear and hope together in one package, a ligament, a twine, a hinge was necessary – linking life that is bound to end, and soon, to the world that is bound to last, forever.

Ivan, the most 'intellectual' of Fyodor Dostoevsky's Karamazov brothers, knew how difficult it is to live with an awareness of eternity, but he knew no less how difficult it is to be human without it . . . According to another highly educated character in the same novel, Rakitin, Ivan averred that love was against Nature, and if it happened and went on happening among humans, it was solely thanks to the belief of humans in their own immortality.[8] Once they lose that faith, 'not just love will dry up, but all that vital élan that prompts them to stay alive. Moreover, nothing will then be immoral, anything will be allowed, even cannibalism . . .' Stop believing in God and immortality, replace faith with reason – and selfishness becomes the sole sensible rule. 'Without immortality, no goodness', Ivan admits, when pressed to reveal his convictions.

Of Rakitin himself, Ivan's brother Dimitri reports that in his opinion the 'wise man is allowed all'. 'Chemistry, brother, chemistry. Nothing doing, Your Highness [God] – step aside, chemistry marches on.'

What will happen once all humans get rid of God and eternity (as happen it must, with the merciless logic of successive geological layers) is that man will concentrate on 'taking from life everything it may give, for the sake of happiness and joy, but only in this world, here and now'. By then humans will themselves become 'like gods', imbued with divine spirit and 'titanic conceit'. Knowledge that life is but a fleeting moment, that a second chance is not on offer, will change the nature of love. Love will have no time to dwell. What it loses in duration, it will gain in intensity. It will burn more dazzlingly than ever, aware of being doomed to be lived through and used up in a single moment and right to the bottom instead of spreading flatly and thinly, as before, over eternity and the immortal life of the soul . . .

This is, let us note, Satan speaking for a change, when visiting Ivan in his nightmare.

Nightmare? Why nightmare? Because millennia will be needed for the whole of humanity to wise up and reach the sagacity so far only in the possession of Satan, and the learned few . . . While the rest of mankind will go on wallowing in their superstitions and groping through the dark corridors of eternity, those enlightened few will become gods – not like the *immortal* gods among the mortals, but like *free* gods in the world of slaves. For 'there is no law for God! Where God stands – there is God's place! Where I'll stand, will be the first place . . . "Everything goes" – and that is it!'

Perhaps there is a paradise of passionate love waiting at the end of the road to reason's wisdom. But it may take millennia to travel that road. And in the meantime, while treading it, mile by mile, year by year – the hell. Can hell be the road to paradise? And is the paradise worth the millennia of hell?

This is the sort of questions the learned men like Ivan Karamazov or Rakitin (or, indeed, Satan) keep asking and are tormented by. In the Jewish tradition, though, at some point in history the age of prophecy, and so of God speaking to humans, ended. (At the threshold of the modern era, Pascal would rediscover that end in his idea of *Deus absconditus*. Once the authority of the church as the collective mediator between God and humans began to fade, the humans found out that there was no answer to their calls and no audible voice at the other end of the line.) As Larry Jay Young puts it, 'God decided to close a formerly open channel of communication. No one really understood why.' Was He offended, disenchanted and repelled by his insubordinate, wayward, prank-addicted creation? Or did he wish to put His creation to a test, see how well (or badly) instructed human creatures were and how they could cope with the temptations, and the repulsiveness, of the world He had cast them in? Or perhaps the fact that the direct line went dead was only

> God's way of telling us that we no longer need Him to hover around us, and comment upon our every move . . . God must believe that we are able to stand on our own two feet, and do justice to one another, and to the world that has been left to our care. The only remaining question is whether or not human beings prove themselves worthy of God's confidence.[9]

The ultimate meaning of the 'end of the age of prophecy' is that we, human beings, are condemned to choice, a choice without certainty that it will prove in the end to be the right choice, and a choice that will nevertheless have to be made again and again, since there is no inkling as to how (and whether!) the curse of uncertainty can be blotted out. Orphaned by the authoritative 'no-doubt-left' and 'no-disobedience-allowed' command, smarting under the cruelty of the verdict and the resulting enormity of their task, humans have called 'Paradise' that easy-going, happy-go-lucky condition of no-need–to-choose and freedom from the premonition that deeds may be good *or* evil.

It was at the dawn of modernity that *Deus* was found *absconditus*. And it was at the dawn of modernity that culture was discovered and found to have been hiding behind the speaking God. It was now up to the culture made by and being made by humans to take over the task of linking mortal life with the world's eternity and to distil (as Baudelaire would have put it) crumbs of solidity and duration out of the impetuous flow of transient human accomplishments.

Nowadays, all waiting, any procrastination, all delays turn into a stigma of inferiority.

The drama of power hierarchy is daily restaged (with the secretaries and personal assistants, but ever more often the security guards, cast in the role of stage managers) in innumerable entrance lobbies and waiting rooms, where some (inferior) people are asked 'to take a seat' and kept waiting until some other (superior) people are 'free to see them now'. The badge of privilege (arguably, one of the most potent stratifying factors) is the access to shortcuts, to the means of making the gratification instantaneous. Position in the hierarchy is measured by skill (or ineptitude) in reducing or cutting out completely the timespan separating a want from its fulfilment. Climbing the social hierarchy is measured by rises in the ability to have what one wants (whatever it may be) *now* – without delay.

Let us recall: 'eternity' is a work of the imagination. That work starts from the experience of the 'long term' – of a long, long time ahead, with the end nowhere in sight; of things and people being and staying around, with little inclination to fall apart or vanish from view. That work starts from such an experience: from an endlessly, monotonously repeated experience of the 'it (she/he) is always there', 'it (she/he) won't go away'. It is from experience like this of faces and places, routines and rituals, sights and sounds which are familiar, stay familiar and are expected to remain as familiar as they are now that the idea of 'eternity' is formed. But there is little such experience left now – in the quicksands of protean, kaleidoscopic sights. There is little left around, inside everybody's *Lebenswelt*, that can be called 'reliable', let alone 'rock solid'.

A friend of mine living in one of the European Union countries, a highly intelligent, superbly educated, uniquely creative person with full command of several languages, who would pass most job tests and interviews with flying colours, complained in a private letter of the 'labour market being as frail as gossamer and as brittle as china'. For two years she worked, with the full measure of the usual ups and down of market fortunes, as a freelance translator and legal adviser. A single mother, she yearned for a more regular income and so opted for steady employment with a salary cheque every month. For one and a half years she worked for a company briefing budding entrepreneurs on the intricacies of state and EU law, but as new business was slow in coming the company promptly went bankrupt. For another year and a half she worked for the Ministry of Agriculture, running a section dedicated to the development of contacts with the newly independent Baltic countries. Come the next election, the new government coalition chose to cede that worry to private initiative and so disbanded the department. The next job lasted only half a year: the State Board of Ethnic Equality followed the pattern of governmental cuts and declared her redundant.

The spectacular story, less than twenty years long, of the breathtaking rise and mind-boggling collapse of the marketing giant Enron has been well documented. Led by its new managers (Kenneth Lay first, Jeffrey Skilling later), it rose almost overnight from a rather unadventurous provincial gas-selling firm to one runaway success after another and was universally lauded by leading economists and financial experts for its insatiable hunger for economic growth ('Lay and Skilling were cast as heroes of deregulation and apostles of the free market' and admired for holding fast to a 'ruthless sink-or-swim philosophy,' as Conal Walsh sums up the dominant opinion of the day),[10] only to be shortly afterwards equally unanimously decried and disowned by the same authorities. Much less discussed (because less unique and

sensational, but much more common) was the impact of Ronald
Reagan's deregulation policy (in which 'Enron saw its chance and
took it') on the plight, morale, worldviews and life strategies
of the successively hired and fired cohorts of Enron employees.
Applicants for jobs 'were put through a rigorous screening process
and had to demonstrate a strong sense of urgency in everything
they did'. Indeed – in *everything*. This was not a matter of a one-
off test – life in Enron was a day-in, day-out test, the pressure
never relenting. No credit of trust accrued, the memory of the
most impressive success would hardly survive to the next morning
unless yesterday's 'killing' was followed by another, yet more
dazzling. 'Twice a year 15 per cent of the workforce was ritually
sacked to be replaced by new arrivals. And a further 30 per cent
warned to improve.' The dedication of the employees, 'old' and
brand new, had to be absolute – but was bound to be short-lived.
Enron was not a plot on which to build lifelong plans: just a
camping site for portable tents easy to pitch and easier yet to fold.
Life in the company constantly hovered on the brink of redundancy and felt like a daily rehearsal of waste disposal. Everyone's
turn to be disposed of was never far away, and so by the time it
arrived it could be greeted in most cases as a welcome relief of
tension rather than a random blow of fate. 'The company's cut-
throat working culture' 'destroyed the morale and internal cohesion' of its employees. It also eroded their power to resist the
prospect of being assigned to waste and the state of affairs that
made such prospects real. The only lasting heirloom such employees will take home when the time to clear their desk comes, as it
surely will, sooner rather than later, is the sober but no doubt
helpful knowledge of just how thin and frail is the line separating
a seat of power from a rubbish heap, a moment of glory from
humiliating defeat, a badge of honour from the stigma of disgrace
and a warm embrace from cold rejection.

As a matter of fact, they are likely to carry with them something else as well: two important lessons they've learned.

Lesson one: days count as much as, and not a bit more than,
the satisfaction you can cream off them. The prize you can real-
istically hope and work for is a *different today*, not a *better tomorrow*. The future is beyond your (and anybody else's, for that

matter) grasp, so stop looking for the pot of gold at the end of the rainbow. 'Long term' worries are for the gullible and improvident. As the French say: *le temps passe vite, il faut profiter de la vie . . .* So try to enjoy as much as you can in the intervals between trips to the rubbish heaps.

Lesson two: whatever else you do, keep your options open. Oaths of loyalty are for the same hapless guys who worry about the 'long term'. Do not commit yourself for longer than absolutely necessary. Keep your engagements shallow and thin so that they can be torn away leaving no wound and no scars. Loyalty and commitments, like all the other utilities, have their 'use by' date. Don't keep them a moment longer.

The experience of Enron's men and women could not be as unique as the publicity that followed its abrupt end suggested: if it were, research institutes around the affluent world would not be as busy as they are (according to a recent *Village Voice* report)[11] searching for a drug likely to cure or alleviate 'post-traumatic stress disorder' (PTSD); there must be a wide market waiting for the invention. At the Ponce School of Medicine in Puerto Rico scientists are trying to help the brain to 'unlearn' fear and inhibitions; at Harvard University they are experimenting with propranolol pills as a means to 'nip the effects of trauma in the bud'. Researchers at the Irvine campus of the University of California have already succeeded in inhibiting hormonal reactions to fear in rats – 'softening the formation of memories and emotions they evoke'. What next? One possibility is of a soldier causing 'flames and screaming, deafening blasts and unforgettably acrid air' and walking through a ground 'littered with broken bodies of women and children' and then rushing 'back to start popping pills that can, over the course of two weeks, immunize him against a lifetime of crushing remorse'. And so the soldier would be able to start all over again. While the researchers stay strictly neutral about the causes of PTSD, they defend the morality of their research and its hoped-for results; the drugs will salvage those who 'made the killing' (be they the soldiers or Enron traders) from the trauma that would condemn them to the wastage tip. Objectors point out that this will only make the immoral practice of confining humans to waste and their swift and radical disposal all the easier and less costly, and therefore more tempting. To which the likely response will be that the job of the researchers is 'to prevent the onset of a disease, not change the social circumstances that bring it about'.

Interviewed by Oliver Burkman of the *Guardian*, an eighteen-year old English girl declared her dad, a teacher, to be her anti-hero: 'I don't want to look back on my life and see that I went into a job because it was safe and stayed there forever.'[12] Dads who have stuck to their jobs for life (if there are such dads still around, that is) are viewed by their offspring as a warning and a deterrent: this is the kind of life we must do whatever we can to avoid. While a New York baker complained to Richard Sennett about the dads' side of the value conflict: 'You can't imagine how stupid I feel when I talk to my kids about commitment. It's an abstract virtue to them, they don't see it anywhere.'[13] To be sure, there is little convincing evidence of the blessings of commitment that could be gleaned from the dads' biographies. They might have tried to commit themselves to something more solid and durable than themselves – a vocation, a cause, a workplace – only to find that there were few if any solid and durable takers willing to accept their offer of a lifelong commitment.

Running after things and catching them in full flight while they are still fresh and fragrant – that is 'in'. Procrastination, settling for what is there already, is 'out'. 'In' or 'out' also applies to the followers of such opposite strategies. Professor John Kotter, of Harvard Business School, advises his readers to avoid being entangled in long-term employment of the 'tenure track' sort; indeed, developing institutional loyalty and becoming too tightly engrossed in any given job for a long time to come is ill-advised when 'business concepts, product designs, competitor intelligence, capital equipment and *all kinds of knowledge* have shorter credible life spans' (italics added).[14]

Benjamin Franklin's discovery that 'time is money' was an accolade for time: time is a value, time is important, something to be cherished and cared for, just as your capital and your investments are. The contemporary 'impatience syndrome' conveys an opposite message: time is a bore and a chore, a pain, a snub to human freedom and a challenge to human rights, none of which must or needs to be suffered gladly. Time is a thief. Agree to wait, to delay the rewards due for your patience – and you'll be robbed of the chance of joys and pleasures that are in the habit of coming once and then disappearing forever. The passage of time is to be recorded on the debit side of human life projects; it brings losses, not gains. The passage of time portends the waste of opportunities that ought to have been grasped and consumed as they came.

Waiting is a shame, and the shame of waiting rebounds on the one who waits. Waiting is something to be ashamed of because it may be noted and taken as evidence of indolence or low status, seen as a symptom of rejection and a signal to exclude. The suspicion of not being really in demand, an intuition never too far from the level of consciousness, now rises to the surface and causes numerous ripples: Why must I wait for what I desire/covet? Do my wishes count as much as they deserve? Are they as respected as they should be? Am I truly needed and welcome? Or am I snubbed? If so, is this snub a hint that I am already on the way out? Am I next on the redundancy list secretly plotted by those who keep me waiting?

A vicious circle, if ever there was one. The vertiginous pace of change devalues everything that might be desirable and desired today, marking it from the start as the waste of tomorrow, whereas the fear of one's own wastage that oozes from the life experience of the dizzying pace of change prompts desires to be more avid and change to be more quickly desired . . .

'Debt becomes the norm for the middle classes,' conclude the authors of a study initiated and supervised by Lucy Purdy from Publicis.[15] It was expected that more than £1.7 billion of credit card spending over Christmas of 2002 won't be paid by the end of January 2003 and so will increase further the already unprecedented burden of debt. As Frances Walker of the Consumer Credit Counselling Service informs us, the average client/patient seeking help now owes about £24,000 – 5 per cent more than last year. British consumers, like British politics, seem to follow where the Americans as usual have pioneered: the total consumer debt of American households rose from $200 billion in 1964 to $7,200 billion in 2002; by the end of 2002, it reached 40 per cent of total individual income.[16]

Three out of five people interviewed by Publicis researchers admitted that they went into debt because they bought things which they later regretted buying; one in three admits buying things they could not really afford. They found the temptation impossible to resist. The authors of the report advise such victims of desire: 'If you can't resist a sale, decide in advance that you'll only stay for 15 or 30 minutes.' In other words, slice the time of thinking even thinner; the longer the time you spend weighing your decisions, the more you risk. The cure for the bane of 'short-termism' in the search for pleasure is a shorter term yet . . .

The authors of that report quote a credo expounded by a 29-year-old designer from Leeds: 'I believe in living for the moment. I just think if I want something now I'm not going to save up for a year: I'll buy on a credit card . . . Rather than stay in and begrudge myself something, I'll put it on credit.' And a frank and sober admission by a 28-year-old civil servant from Winchester: 'You get your first credit card and max it out. Then you get another in order to pay off the first. After a while it all becomes like Monopoly money. You start to think: "I already owe £20,000, so what's another £200 going to be?"' And another resigned admission: 'If you lived within your means, you'd never do anything.'

Lucy Purdy attempts to explain the findings: 'General dissatisfaction has led us to become very indulgent and impatient in our personal lives. We want to improve our lot now. As a result we are going into debt. Most important, debt appears to have lost any adverse moral implications.'

Curiously, astonishingly, bafflingly, buying on credit is the sole form of longish-term commitment which the denizens of the liquid modern world do not just tolerate and endure but enter joyously. They even begin to see going into debt as a benign sort of commitment that helps to fight and conquer its other, malignant varieties. A belief which the credit card companies wholeheartedly endorse, promising to take over and 'repay' what you owe to other credit card companies . . . There is not much logic in all that, but then who except its hired or voluntary bards said that consumer society thrives on logic and logic-guided conduct by its customers?

Why are credit and the chance of going into debt felt to be so badly needed, are so eagerly offered and so gladly and gratefully accepted? The simple, off-the-cuff and also, as we have seen above, most common answer is: to speed up and bring closer the satisfaction of needs, desires or wants. On second thoughts, however (though the whirlwind pace of the offer-and-demand game seldom allows for second thoughts), the major service rendered by the easy availability of credit is to make easier the disposal of things no longer needed, desired and wanted. Think again, and you'll see that once buying on credit and living in debt become norms ('You are regarded as financially naive if you're not in debt'; going into debt 'appears to be regarded as a clever thing to do,' observes Neil Scaife, one of the Publicis researchers), they dig even deeper into the modality of consumer life. They may speed up the birth of new desires and shorten the way between the birth of a desire and its satisfaction – but they also speed up the fading of desires and their replacement with resentment and rejection. All in all, they shorten the lifespan of the objects of desire and smooth and speed their travel to the rubbish heap. With credit and debt facilities constantly within reach, why should you wish to hold on to something that 'does not give you full satisfaction' (whatever that 'full satisfaction' may mean)? Credit and debt are midwives of waste, and in that role rests the deepest cause of their spectacular career in the society of consumers.

Of Los Angeles, the city in whose pattern most residents of other cities would dearly wish to remake their own, Michelle Ogundehin writes that it has 'a knack for taking today's fame and turning it into tomorrow's forgotten fad'.[17] Recently, the Los Angeles architectural company Marmol Radziner and Associates shot to instant fame thanks to the (astonishing, shocking and utterly fanciful by their city's standards) idea of stripping a 1946 house, until recently the residence of Barry Manilow, of the several layers of later fashions – and restoring it to its pristine, but since long scorned and forgotten, 'Modern Style' shape. This spectacular display of the waste-recycling art must have struck a sensitive

chord; at least for a moment, the two partners set the pattern of
taste for the city's rich. They now 'subscribe to a romantic notion':
they dream of 'something timeless'. Timeless? What they dream
of is 'to build beautiful buildings that will still be standing in 20
years' time'.

In the lifestyle magazines the columns dedicated to 'what is
new' or 'what is in' (what you must have, do, and be seen having
and doing) sit next to the columns devoted to 'what is out' and
what you must not have or do, nor be seen having or doing.
Information on the latest fashions comes in a package deal
with the news of the latest waste: the second part of the information package grows in size from one issue of the magazine to
another.

Caroline Roux admits (under the title 'The look of 2003', so
be warned – perhaps when you read these words the information
below will be sorely out of date): 'I didn't ask for interiors to fall
victim to the same vicious turnover as fashion, but they have. And
if you wouldn't be seen dead in last year's Burberry, why would
you want to invest in last year's flooring?' And so, for instance,
'those big bowls of lilies have to go. They're old-style glamour.'
'Don't indulge yourself with any more translucent plastics.'
'Huge contemporary statement sofas just aren't the answer.'
'Rubbers and linos are a bit last season.' And then comes the final
shot, lest readers wrongly sniff an air of finality in these verdicts
and assume that they have got all the wisdom they need and that
the time for a welcome rest has arrived: 'Right now, I'd opt for a
second-hand parquet. But ask me again in six months.'[18]

Peter Paphides wistfully remembers the seven-inch singles of
yore: short-play records offering the kind of blissful experience
our contemporaries covet, without excessively taxing their capital
of time and emotions. One possible interpretation of that nostal-
gic tone is that only now have we matured enough to appreciate
how far the Oldies were ahead of their time – speaking past our
ears straight to the kind of life we live now and meeting the standards we struggle to observe today. 'There is something honest
about a single. It's selling you a song, that's it. It won't outstay its
welcome.' 'The single is a cheap date. It demands little commitment. All it asks for is some of your pocket money.'[19] You may

say: easy come, easy go. You won't feel much pain when it is time to let it go; this thought is comforting. Mind you: this date does not demand *commitment*. It is but a date . . . Dates last as long as they last. They end the moment they end.

The point is, though, that even a 'cheap date' will tax you heavily once it turns from a rare festive delight into a lasting compulsion – when it begets a lifelong routine. This is where credit cards and debt facilities come in. They take, as the banks issuing them promise, the waiting out of wanting. But they also (though credit card companies are less sincere about that) take the guilt out of the waste disposal; the spiritual torments out of parting ways; the danger of an outstayed welcome out of a casual encounter. You can now handle all dates, however expensive, as if they were cheap . . .

Beauty, alongside happiness, has been one of the most exciting modern promises and guiding ideals of the restless modern spirit. The convoluted history and semantic adventures of the dream of happiness were briefly described by me elsewhere.[20] Now comes the turn of beauty; its history may be seen as paradigmatic for the birth and development of the liquid modern culture of waste.

The concepts that cropped up most often in the early stages of the modern debate about 'what is beautiful' were harmony, proportion, symmetry, order and suchlike – all converging on the ideal most pithily formulated by Leone Battista Alberti: the ideal of an arrangement in which any further change could only be a change for the worse; a state of things to which Alberti gave the name of *perfection*. Beauty meant perfection; and it was the perfect that had the right to be called beautiful. Many a great modern artist struggled to conjure up such a state of perfection: indeed, to make the search of perfection in Alberti's sense the principal subject-matter of their work. Think for instance of Mondrian, Matisse, Arp or Rothko . . . Cut the colourful rectangles out of Mondrian's paintings and attempt to rearrange them in an order different from the one Mondrian selected – and the odds are that you'll find your arrangements, indeed *all and any* alternative arrangements, inferior – less pleasing, 'ugly' by comparison . . . Or cut out the figures of Matisse's *Dancers* and try to relate them to each other in a different way: you will most certainly experience a similar frustration.

But what, in the last account, is the significance of 'perfection'? Once the object has acquired the 'perfect' form, all further change is undesirable and inadvisable. Perfection means that change has fulfilled its purpose and now should come to an end. No more changes. From now on, everything will be the same – forever. What is perfect will never lose its value, never become redundant, will never be disposed of and so will never turn into waste – instead it is all further search and experimenting that will from now on be redundant. And so, when pining after perfection, we need to stretch our imagination to the utmost, deploy all our creative powers – but only in order to make imagination in the end a wasteful pastime and creativity not just unnecessary, but undesirable . . . If beauty means perfection, and if reaching perfection is the purpose of the search, then once beauty has been attained nothing is going to happen any more. There is nothing *after* beauty.

Let me repeat what was said at the beginning of this chapter: we, human beings, are, and cannot help being, 'transgressive', 'transcending' animals. We live ahead of the present. Our representations may be cut loose from the senses and run ahead of them. The world that we inhabit is always a step, or a mile, or a stellar year ahead of the world we are experiencing. That part of the world sticking out of lived experience we call 'ideals'. The mission of ideals is to guide us into the territory as yet unexplored and unmapped.

'Beauty' is one of the ideals that guide us beyond the world that already is. Its value is fully encapsulated in its guiding power. Had we ever reached it, it would have lost that power, and so also its value. Our journey would have come to an end. There would be nothing left to transgress and transcend, and so also no human life as we know it. But perhaps, thanks to language and to imagination made both possible and inevitable by language, that point can never be reached.

We call many things 'beautiful', but there is no object which we call by that name of which we will honestly say that it cannot be improved. 'Perfection' *is forever 'not yet'*, a step or more ahead, reached for, but not really grasped. Indeed, a state of affairs in which no further improvement will be desirable may be dreamed of only by people who have a lot to improve. The *vision* of perfection may be a eulogy of stillness, but the *job* of that vision is to pull and push us away from what is, to bar us from standing still . . . *Stillness* is what graveyards are about – and yet, paradoxically, it is the *dream of stillness* that keeps us alive and the living busy. As long as the dream remains unfulfilled, we count days and the days count: there is a purpose and there is an unfinished job to do . . . As the great Polish scientist Maria Curie-Skłodowska confided to her brother, with a mixture of pride and shame, one never notices what has been done; one can only see what remains to be done . . .

Not that such work, stubbornly, infuriatingly refusing to be finished, is an unmixed blessing and brings unpolluted happiness. The condition of 'unfinished business' has many charms, but like all other conditions it is short of perfection . . .

As the great Italian sociologist Alberto Melucci used to say, 'We are plagued by the fragility of the presentness which calls for a firm foundation where none exists.' And so, 'when contemplating change, we are always torn between desire and fear, between anticipation and uncertainty.'[21] This is it: *uncertainty*. Or, as Ulrich Beck prefers to call it, *risk*: that unwanted, awkward and vexing, but stubborn, obtrusive, undetachable companion (or stalker rather?!) of all anticipation – a sinister spectre haunting the inveterate decision-makers that we are. For us, as Melucci pithily put it, 'choice became a destiny.'

'Became' is not perhaps a correct expression: after all, for the reasons already spelled out, humans were choosers as long as they were humans. But it can be said that at no other time was the necessity to make choices so deeply felt and to such frightful effect, daily and under conditions of painful yet incurable uncertainty, with the purposes of action and the standards of proceeding hardly ever lasting as long as it would take to reach the purpose and complete the action, with the constant threat of being 'left behind', 'not up to new demands' and (horror of horrors) thrown out of the game. What separates the present-day agony of choice from the discomforts that have tormented the *homo eligens*, the 'man choosing', at all times is precisely the gnawing suspicion or

painful discovery that there are no clear-cut rules and trustworthy, universally approved objectives that may release the choosers
completely, or at least in part, from their responsibility for the
adverse – misconceived or unforeseen – consequences of their
choices. There are no unmistakable orientation points or foolproof
guidelines, and such reference points and guidelines as seem trustworthy today are likely to be debunked tomorrow as misleading
or corrupt.

Indeed, everything around in the 'really existing world' seems
to be only 'until further notice'. In 2000, Donald Rumsfeld is a
director of the powerful European engineering company ABB that
sells the North Korean government designs and key components
for nuclear reactors; around Christmas 2002 Donald Rumsfeld,
the US Defense Secretary, declares North Korea a 'terrorist regime
. . . on the verge of collapse', and a few months later, after the fall
of Baghdad, calls it to draw the 'appropriate lesson'.[22] Allegedly
rock-solid companies are unmasked as figments of accountants'
imaginations. Whatever is 'good for you' today may be reclassified
tomorrow as your poison. Apparently firm commitments and
solemnly signed agreements may be overturned overnight. And
promises, or most of them, seem to be made solely to be betrayed
and broken. There seems to be no stable, secure island among the
tides. To quote Melucci once more, 'We no longer possess a home;
we are repeatedly called upon to build and then rebuild one, like
the three little pigs of the fairy tale, or we have to carry it along
with us on our backs like snails.'

To sum it all up: at no other time has Robert Louis Stevenson's
memorable verdict that 'to travel hopefully is a better thing than
to arrive' sounded truer than it does in our liquidized and fluid
modern world. When destinations move or lose their charm faster
than legs can walk, cars drive or planes fly, keeping on the move
matters more than the destination. Not making a habit of anything practised at the moment, not being tied up by the legacy
of one's past, wearing one's current identity as one wears shirts
that may be promptly replaced when they fall out of use or out
of fashion, rejecting past lessons and abandoning past skills with
no inhibitions or regret – these are all becoming the hallmarks of
present-day, liquid modern life politics and attributes of liquid

modern rationality. Liquid modern culture no longer feels like a culture of learning and accumulation like the cultures recorded in the historians' and ethnographers' reports. It looks instead like a *culture of disengagement, discontinuity and forgetting*.

In this kind of culture and in the life-political strategies that it values and promotes, there is not much room for ideals. There is even less room for ideals that prompt a long-term, continuous and sustained effort of small steps leading hopefully towards admittedly distant results. And there is no room at all for an ideal of perfection, deriving all its allurement from the promise of *the end* of choosing, changing, improving. To be more precise, such an ideal may still hover above the lifeworld of a liquid modern man or woman – but only as a dream, a dream no longer expected to come true and when it comes to the nitty-gritty seldom wished to come true; a night-dream that all but dissipates in the light of day.

This is why beauty, in its orthodox meaning of an ideal to strive for and to die for, seems to have fallen on hard times.

In what George Steiner called 'casino culture', every cultural product is calculated for maximal impact (that is, for breaking up, pushing out and disposing of the cultural products of yesterday) and instant obsolescence (that is, shortening the distance between the novelty and the rubbish bin, being wary of outstaying its welcome and quickly vacating the stage so that nothing should stand in the way of the cultural products of tomorrow). The artists who once identified the value of their work with eternal duration and so struggled for a perfection which would put an end to change and therefore would be assured of eternity, now excel in installations meant to be dismantled when the exhibition closes, in happenings that will end the moment the actors decide to turn the other way, in wrapping up bridges until the traffic is restarted and unfinished buildings until the building work is resumed, and in 'space sculptures' that invite nature to take its toll and supply another proof, if another proof were needed, of the ludicrous brevity of all human deeds and the transience of their traces. No one is expected, let alone encouraged, to remember today yesterday's talk-of-the-town, though no one is expected, let alone allowed, to steer clear of the talk-of-the-town of today.

To be admitted to the casino culture of the liquid modern era, one needs to be unchoosy and omnivorous, refrain from defining one's taste too strictly and from sticking to any taste for long, to be ready to try and to enjoy everything currently on offer and be anything but consistent and stable in one's preferences. Rejection of the new is in bad taste, and she or he who rejects risks risks rejection. But equally incorrect and dangerous is loyalty to the old. And the ageing of the new, once a long process, takes ever less time. 'New' tends to turn into 'old', to be bypassed and overtaken, instantaneously.

Imperceptibly, the meaning of 'beauty' undergoes a fateful change. In the current usages of the word, philosophers would hardly recognize the concepts they so earnestly and laboriously constructed over centuries. More than anything else, they would miss the link between beauty and eternity, aesthetic value and durability. However furiously they quarrelled, all philosophers used to agree once (mind you, *in the past!*) that beauty rises above fickle and fragile private whims, and that even if there could be 'beauty at first sight', it was the flow of time that would put it to the only trustworthy – the ultimate and clinching – test. Today's philosophers would also miss the 'claim to universal validity' that used to be viewed as an indispensable attribute of any properly aesthetic judgement. It is those two attributes that fell by the wayside with the advent of 'casino culture' and are conspicuously absent from the current popular usages of the word 'beauty'.

The consumer market and the pattern of conduct that it requires and cultivates are adapted to the liquid modern 'casino culture', which in turn is adapted to that market's pressures and seductions. The two chime well with each other; they feed on and mutually reinforce each other. Not to waste their clients' time, or prejudice or pre-empt their future and yet unpredictable joys, consumer markets offer products meant for immediate consumption, preferably for one-off use, rapid disposal and replacement, so that living spaces won't stay cluttered once the objects admired and coveted today fall out of fashion. The clients, confused by the whirlwind of fashion, the mind-boggling variety of offers and the vertiginous pace of their change, can no longer rely on being able to learn and memorize – and so they must (and do, gratefully) accept the reassurances that the product currently on offer is '*the thing*', the '*hot* thing', the '*must have*' and the thing they '*must be seen (in or with)*'.

The 'objective', everlasting or universal aesthetic value of the product is the last thing to worry about. But neither is the beauty 'in the eye of the beholder'. Beauty is instead located in today's fashion, and so the beautiful is bound to turn ugly the moment the current fashion is replaced, as it surely will soon be. Were it not for the market's wondrous capacity of imposing a regular, even if short-lived, pattern on the ostensibly individual and so potentially random and diffuse customer choices, customers would feel totally disoriented and lost. Taste is no longer a safe guide, learning and relying on already acquired knowledge is a trap rather than a help, yesterday's *comme il faut* may well turn without warning into *comme il ne faut pas*.

'Beauty rules,' observes Yves Michaud in his trenchant report on the state of the arts in the liquid modern world. 'In all respects it has become an imperative: be beautiful, or at least spare us your ugliness.'[23] To be ugly means to be condemned to the rubbish tip. Conversely, having been condemned to the rubbish bin is all the proof one needs of ugliness.

The 'rule of beauty' was, wasn't it, what modern artists and the learned philosophers of aesthetics who reflected on their labours dreamed of all along? So what do we witness: the final triumph of the beautiful? The fulfilment of at least one of the many ambitious 'modern projects'?

Not so, Michaud would say. In fact, aesthetics has triumphed – but over its own object . . . Aesthetics won by making works of art ('precious and rare', 'invested with aura and magic qualities', 'unique, refined and sublime') redundant. 'The "aesthetic" is nowadays cultivated, spread, distributed, consumed in a world emptied of works of art.' Art has evaporated into an 'aesthetic ether' of sorts, which like the ether of the pioneers of modern chemistry permeates all things indiscriminately and condenses in none. 'Beautiful' are those jumpers with the currently celebrated designer's label; bodies reshaped in gyms and through plastic surgery and make-up after the latest fashion; packaged products on supermarket shelves. 'Even the corpses are beautiful – neatly

wrapped in plastic covers and aligned in front of the ambulances.'
Everything has, or at least may have and should try to have, its
fifteen minutes, even perhaps fifteen days, of beauty on the road
to the refuse tip.

We may say that what graveyards are to living human beings,
museums are to the life of the arts: sites to dispose of the objects
that are no longer vital and animated. Some human corpses are
laid in graves and overlaid with gravestones to be visited by those
who feel orphaned or bereaved by their disappearance; some
others have vanished forever in unmarked mass burial places or
disintegrated without trace in scorched villages, burning ovens
and the depths of Rio de la Plata. Some works of art are placed
in museums, where their once acclaimed beauty has been sani-
tized, sterilized and embalmed, to be preserved, alongside archae-
ological excavation sites, for the eyes of lovers of history or
passengers of tourist coaches. Graveyards and museums alike are
set away from the hurly-burly of daily life, separated from the
business of life in their own enclosed space with their own visiting hours. In museums, as in cemeteries, one does not talk out
loud, does not eat, drink, run, or touch the objects of the visit,
and one keeps children on a leash.

The scene of daily life is different. It is the site of aesthetics,
not *objets d'art*. It is the stage of ephemeral performances and happenings, of installations scrambled together from manifestly and
self-consciously perishable materials or sewn together out of the
patches of immaterial thoughts. Nothing put and seen on that
stage is meant to last or be conserved when its time is over – frailty
and transience are the names of the game. Whatever happens
there can carry only as much meaning as its own tiny carrying
capacity can admit and hold. That meaning will after all be sought
and gleaned by people drilled in the art of zapping – and 'zappers'
enter 'after the editor and before "the end" appears on the
screen'.[24] Michaud writes of the 'new regime of attention which
privileges scanning over reading and the deciphering of meanings.
The image is fluid and mobile, less a spectacle or a datum than
an element of a chain of action.' Having cut itself loose from the
referential sequence of which it was a part, 'the image is free to
be harnessed at will to any cortège or sequence of phantasms.'

The reallocation of images from being viewed in focus to the attention's own refuse tip – irrelevance and invisibility – is random. The difference between 'the object' and its indifferent surroundings has been all but obliterated, much as has the time separating the moment of being in focus from that of being cast out of sight. Objects and waste change places easily. In a Copenhagen art gallery I admired an installation put together from a series of TV screens with huge captions: 'The Promised Land'. I found the installation thoughtful and thought-provoking – not least because of the broom and bucket standing in the corner at the end of the series of images. Before I had time, though, to think its meaning through to the end, a cleaner came to collect her tools she had put in the corner for the duration of the coffee break.

Only statistics may offer perplexed viewers, lost on their search for beauty, a rescue from the chaos conjured up by free-floating aesthetics with no fixed objects. Salvation is in numbers. All those people who proudly sport the latest tokens cannot be simultaneously wrong . . . Magically, the massiveness of choice ennobles its object. That object *must* be beautiful, otherwise it would not have been chosen by so many choosers. Beauty is in high sales figures, box-office records, platinum discs, sky-high television ratings (Andy Warhol once mused: imagine a bunch of banknotes hanging on a string – 160,000 dollars . . . What a beautiful picture!). Perhaps beauty is also somewhere else, as some philosophers stubbornly insist – but how would you know? And who would approve of your findings, if you searched for them in bizarre places *de quoi on ne parle plus*? Even the Old Masters, whose reputation, one would think, is shockproof thanks to their venerable age and the number of tests they have triumphantly passed over the centuries, cannot ignore the new rules of the beauty game. It is Vermeer today, Matisse the other day and Picasso the day after that 'you must see and be seen to be seeing', depending on the latest hyped and 'everybody who is anybody is talking about' exhibition. As in all other cases, beauty is not a quality of their canvases but the (quantitatively evaluated) quality of the *event*.

In our liquid modern society, beauty has met the same fate suffered by all the other ideals that used to motivate human restlessness and rebellion. The search for ultimate harmony and eternal duration has been recast as simply an ill-advised concern. Values are values in as far as they are fit for instantaneous, on-the-spot consumption. Values are attributes of *momentary experiences*. And so is beauty. And life is a succession of momentary experiences.

'Beauty has no obvious use; nor is there any clear cultural necessity for it. Yet civilization could not do without it,' Freud mused. 'This useless thing which we expect civilization to value is beauty. We require civilized man to reverence beauty whenever he sees it in nature and to create it in the objects of his handiwork so far as he is able.' Beauty, alongside cleanliness and order, 'obviously occupy a special position among the requirements of civilization'.[25]

Let us note that all three objectives named by Freud as 'the requirements of civilization' are *imaginary horizons* of the civilizing process. It would perhaps be better, less misleading and controversial, to speak instead of *beautification, purification* and *ordering*. We can now see more clearly than earlier generations could possibly see seventy years ago that the 'civilizing process' is not a time-confined transitory period leading to a finished state of civilization, but the very substance of 'civilization'. The idea of a civilization that has completed the effort to civilize (brought to an end the job of cleaning, the bustle of ordering and the search for beauty) is as incongruous as that of a wind that does not blow and a river that does not flow.

It is out of a hunger for beauty that civilizations (that is, the efforts to 'civilize', the 'civilizing processes') have been born. But far from placating that hunger, they seem to have made it insatiable.

'Your car has an MOT every year; so why not your partnership?' asks Hugh Wilson.[26] Indeed. As with the car, so with the partnership. That is, they both make sense only if they satisfy your needs and so long as you are satisfied with the way they do it . . . It would be silly to suppose that they will go on acquitting themselves well in that task for ever and that your satisfaction will be eternal.

Cars age, after all, lose some of their glitter and lustre, stop working – it is no longer enough to stick the key in the ignition to make them work; they need ever more attention to keep them roadworthy. The attention they require becomes both time- and energy-consuming. A law of diminishing returns seems to be at work. At first, the smallest move on your part brings a whole lot of new and unexplored gratifying sensations – but to extract each successive blissful sensation, more and more investment of thought, dedication and labour is needed. Is all that worth your effort? There are so many newer, better cars around, more hand-some, attractive, easier to operate, more responsive. It is time to think of exchange. It is time to consign the old car to waste. Anyway, it was neither destined nor meant to last forever – was it?

We are consumers in a consumers' society. Consumer society is a market society; we are all in and on the market, interchangeably or simultaneously customers and commodities. No wonder that the use/consumption of relationships catches up, and fast, with the pattern of car use/consumption, repeating the cycle that starts from purchase and ends with waste disposal. 'Living together' in Britain lasts on average up to two years. Forty per cent of mar-riages in Britain end in divorce. In the US, the ratio is one in two, and rising. Hugh Wilson aptly suggests that an MOT every year or half-year seems to many people, under the circumstances, a rea-sonable thing to do – as 'taking a relationship in six-month chunks . . . is a part of a trend toward short-term thinking among osten-sibly committed couples.' In the US, the project to institutional-ize marriage contracts that are renewable every two (and at least every ten) years summons ever more vociferous and widespread public support. Wilson quotes Dr Elayne Savage, the author of a book under the tell-tale title *Breathing Room: Creating Space to be a Couple*, to the effect that 'renewable relationships might be the answer for those who are increasingly uncomfortable with total commitment.' Savage approves of that solution, recommending agreements 'up for negotiation' annually, much after the pattern of the 'rolling contracts' rising in popularity on the labour market.

A growing number of observers reasonably expect friends and friendships to play a vital role in our thoroughly individualized

society. With the traditional support structures of social cohesion
fast falling apart, relations woven out of friendship could become
our life-jackets or lifeboats. Ray Pahl, pointing out that in our
times of choice friendship, 'the archetypal social relationship of
choice', is our natural choice, calls friendship the 'social convoy'
of late modern life.[27] Reality seems to be somewhat less straightforward, however. In this 'late modern' or liquid modern life relationships are an ambiguous matter and tend to be the foci of a
most acute and nerve-wracking ambivalence: the price for the
companionship which we all ardently desire is invariably a, partial
at least, surrender of independence, however dearly one would
wish the first without the second . . .

Continuous ambivalence results in cognitive dissonance, a state
of mind notoriously demeaning, incapacitating and difficult to
endure. It invites in turn the usual repertory of mitigating stratagems, among which the marking down, playing down and belit-
tling of one of the two irreconcilable values is the most commonly
resorted to. Subject to contradictory pressures, many a relationship, meant anyway to be only 'until further notice', would snap.
Snapping is a reasonable expectation, something to think of in
advance and be prepared to face. Sensible partners would wish
therefore (as Wilson put it) to 'build in easy "get-out" clauses
from the start'; 'we want the getting-out bit to be as pain-free as
possible.'

When the high likelihood of waste is calculated in the process
of tying relationship bonds, the advice of foresight and prudence
is to take care of the waste disposal facility well in advance. After
all, sober-minded urban developers would not risk starting a building unless a demolition permit was obtained; generals would be
loath to send their troops into battle before a credible exit
scenario was scripted; and employers all around complain that it
is the assumption of their employees' earned rights and the constraints imposed on firing them that make the extension of
employment all but impossible.

Anushka Asthana reports 'the craze of speed dating' (or of a
sort of 'dating conveyor belt') that recently took America, and
London soon after, by storm. 'Eleven tables are placed in a line,
the girls sit down at the one allocated to them and the boys take

turns to face each of them. After three minutes a giant bell rings and, mid-sentence or not, it is time to move on.'[28] If you would like to meet again, you put a tick in the box provided. If the person on the other side of the table feels and does the same, there will be another meeting. If not, this is the end of the story. Adele Testani, president of one company offering this simplified 'skip the inessentials', 'return to the shop if not satisfied', consumer-friendly version of courtship, points out that 'It is now socially acceptable.' Three minutes is enough, because 'you get a sense of what someone is like and can eliminate them if they're wrong.' Most importantly, safety – a guarantee that unless you wish it the three minutes won't turn into three days or months (or, God forbid, years) – is ensured: swapping of phone numbers is not allowed. After instant coffee and instant iced-tea comes instant dating.

What is the attraction of 'speed dating' that overnight made it an astounding commercial success? The opportunity to 'cut out the preliminaries' could be an answer, but it is unlikely to be the only one. Much more important seems to be 'the giant bell' that rings every three minutes and leaves you and your three-minute partner with no choice but to part ways. Negotiating *the start* of companionship is no doubt a complex process calling for courage and skills many may lack (one of Asthana's conversationalists boasted that instead of one date per month, his usual norm, he had in one session 'four dates lined up for the next few weeks'), but negotiating one's way *out of* companionship tends to be a downright traumatic test that taxes spiritual powers in the extreme; and the longer the companionship, the deeper the trauma. Simon Procter, the brain behind another speed-dating company, is clear-sighted and hits the nail on the head: 'If you don't like them, you're out quick.' The waste disposal problem has been solved before it started.

You may say that the other side – agreeing to a date after just a three-minute exchange of glances and sound-bites – is a risky business. It would be if the relationships about to be initiated were intended to last indefinitely. There are only three minutes 'to get to know the love of my life', says the title of the report – and what sort of knowledge can you obtain before the giant bell rings? Fortunately, the kind of partnership most of the speed-dating clients would resolve to enter is a renegotiated contract of the 'return to the shop', from one MOT to another type – and the risk involved in such a relationship is much less harrowing. The bets are carefully hedged all around. With waste disposal outfits in good operating order and instantly available, you can afford the speed.

Speed dating is just one of the rising number of stratagems on offer on the user-friendly market of 'human relations' (more precisely, of their mass produced and inferior but cheaper substitutes). For instance, online personal ads, calculated to cut out even that three-minute-long exposure to the risk of long-term consequences from an imprudent off-the-cuff choice. In the words of Emma Taylor and Lorelei Sharkey, 'if your love life is a bank account, then the personal ad is your cash machine, giving you easy, instant access to whatever you want (casual sex, true love, a bridge partner) whenever you want it.'[29] They could have added that when using a cash machine you enter exactly the sum you are ready to spend and prepared to risk wasting. So the waste, though not completely avoidable, will be calculated in advance and will therefore be less painful. Partners will not complain about costs and irksome sacrifices: meeting through personal ads, they will both know that they are 'both single, both looking' and so – point out Taylor and Sharkey – 'you decide to meet – and boom!'

Barbara Ellen ponders the gains and losses of the emergent 'long-distance relationships.'[30] They offer, she suggests, the opportunity for 'emotional skiving'. We may say that if the long distance is duly kept, the emotions inevitably arising out of a relationship, desirable and welcome as they may be but also threatening to take root and last longer than convenient, are unloaded well before the roots are struck, in periodical short and sharp outbursts, preempting the off-putting moment of wholesale waste disposal. From a tragic and traumatic, nervewracking watershed event, full of acrimony, waste disposal is transformed into a long series of small and relatively painless acts. It is habitualized: regular trips to the dump site are easy and undramatic, almost routine, since they are systematically rehearsed. 'Emotional skiving' in a 'long-distance relationship' therefore has a clear advantage over continuous proximity (dubbed 'presenteeism'): partners may 'skive the boring bits (the rows; the listening) and do all the fun stuff (the sex; the chatting)'.

Partnerships instantly entered, fast consumed and disposed of on demand may however have their side-effects, ones no less painful than the effect of shyness which the speed-dating establishments promise to annul. The spectre of the rubbish heap is never far away. After all, speed and waste disposal services are available to both sides. You may end up in the plight described by Oliver James: poisoned with 'a constant sense of the lack of others in your life, with feelings of emptiness and loneliness akin to bereavement'. You may be 'forever fearful you will be dropped by lovers and friends'. The condition diagnosed here seems to be a natural, logical and rational consequence of a life spattered by instantly fixed and instantly broken partnerships, but James traces its cause to 'dependent depression', an organic or psychical, medical and curable ailment, and suggests that 'the origins of this problem are often in infancy.' 'Unresponsiveness' prompted by 'unempathic relating from the carer' in your childhood 'becomes incorporated into your brain as a set of electrical patterns and chemical levels'.[31] A scientific explanation like this may shift the guilt away from the sufferer and mitigate the degree of self-censure and self-deprecation. Its other effect, though, is an acquittal of the way of life that made the condition named 'dependent depression' such a common affliction.

Confronting that way of life point-blank, let alone challenging it and seeking and joining forces determined to reform it, would certainly prove a long haul: not a proposition that would find many enthusiastic takers inside our culture of speed, instantaneous satisfaction and instant waste disposal. We are trained to seek and expect simpler solutions – and quicker fixes. As in that magic recipe offered by the author of a weekly 'Wellbeing' column writing under the penname of 'Barefoot Doctor': 'just six minutes' practice' will 'make you the most magnetic girl or boy angel on the block'.[32] Six minutes of what? Of a particular way of standing, described by the Barefoot Doctor in minute detail, of 'breathing freely and fluidly', of imagining 'sucking the life-force up through your soles from the ground into your lower belly' . . .

'Four dates lined up for the next few weeks', six minutes of 'sucking the life-force into your lower belly' . . . Tell me what your dreams are, and I'll tell you what you miss most badly and what your fears are. What we all seem to fear, whether suffering from 'dependent depression' or not, whether in the full light of the day or harassed by nocturnal hallucinations, is abandonment, exclusion, being rejected, blackballed, disowned, dropped, stripped of what we are, being refused what we wish to be. We fear being left alone, helpless and hapless. Barred company, loving hearts and helping hands. We fear to be dumped – our turn for the scrapyard. What we miss most badly is the certainty that all that won't happen – not to us. We miss exemption – from the universal and ubiquitous threat of exemption. We dream of immunity against the toxic effluvia of refuse tips.

Horrors of exclusion emanate from two sources, though we are seldom clear about their nature, let alone strive to tell one from the other.

There are the seemingly random, haphazard and utterly unpredictable moves and shifts and drifts of what for the lack of a more precise name are called 'forces of globalization'. They change beyond recognition, and without warning, the familiar landscapes and cityscapes where the anchors of our durable and reliable security used to be cast. They reshuffle people and play havoc with their social identities. They may transform us, from one day to another, into refugees or 'economic migrants'. They may withdraw our certificates of identity or invalidate the identities certified. And they remind us daily that they can do it with impunity – when they dump at our doorsteps those people who have already been rejected, forced to run for their lives or scramble away from home for the means to stay alive, robbed of their identities and self-esteem. We hate those people because we feel that what they are going through in front of our eyes may well prove to be, and soon, a dress rehearsal of our own fate. Trying hard to remove them from our sight – round them up, lock them in camps, deport them – we wish to exorcise that spectre. This is as far as we can go to chase away this sort of horror. We can burn the 'forces of globalization' in effigy only; we seem to have no other ways of evaporating the pent-up anxiety except lighting pyres.

The whole anxiety won't go away in smoke, though – there is too much of it, and the supplies are constantly replenished. The unburnt residue trickles on to another level – that of life politics – where it blends with similar fears reeking from perishing inter-human bonds and disintegrating group solidarities. Following the notorious habits of the Owl of Minerva, there is nothing we talk of with greater solemnity or more relish than of 'networks' of 'connection' or 'relationships', only because the 'real stuff' – the closely knit networks, the firm and secure connections, the fully fledged relationships – has all but fallen apart. As Richard Sennett recently found, in Silicon Valley, the greenhouse of the hottest technologies and the advanced outpost of the current version of the brave new world, the average length of employment in any job is about eight months:[33] and this is a blissful life envied and eagerly emulated throughout the planet.

Thinking long-term under such conditions is obviously out of the question. And where there is no long-term thinking, no 'we will meet again' expectation, there is hardly a sense of shared destiny, a feeling of brotherhood, an urge to join ranks, stand shoulder to shoulder or march in step. Solidarity has little chance of sprouting and striking roots. Relationships are conspicuous mostly by their frailty and superficiality. To quote Sennett again, 'the purely temporary presence in a company prompts people to keep their distance' – to resent closer engagement and beware lasting commitment. Many of us, perhaps most, cannot be sure how long we will stay where we are now and for how long the people with whom we now share the place and interact will stay. If the present bonds may be torn apart at any moment, it seems silly to invest our time and resources in adding to their strength and to put an extra effort into protecting them against wear and tear.

We talk compulsively about networks and try obsessively to conjure them (or at least their phantoms) out of 'speed dating', personal ads and magic incantations of 'messaging' because we painfully miss the safety nets which the true networks of kinship, friends and brothers-in-fate used to provide matter-of-factly, with or without our efforts. Mobile-telephone directories stand for the missing community and are hoped to deputize for the missing inti-macy; they are expected to carry a load of expectations they lack the strength to lift, let alone to hold. As Charles Handy muses, 'fun they may be, these virtual communities, but they create only an illusion of intimacy and a pretence of community.' They are a poor substitute 'for getting your knees under the table, seeing people's faces, and having real conversation'.[34] In an exquisitely insightful study of the cultural consequences of the 'age of insecurity', Andy Hargreaves writes on 'episodic strings of tiny interactions' that are increasingly replacing 'sustained family conversations and relationships'.[35] He quotes Clifford Stoll's opinion that exposed to 'contacts made easy' by electronic technology, we lose the ability to enter into spontaneous interaction with real people.[36]

In fact, we grow shy of face-to-face contacts. We tend to reach for our mobiles and furiously press buttons and knead messages in order to avoid 'making ourselves a hostage to fate' and to escape from the complex, messy, unpredictable – difficult to interrupt and to opt out from – interactions with those 'real people' physically present around us. The wider (even if shallower) our phantom communities of three-minute dating and telephone messaging, the more daunting the task appears of sewing together and holding together the real ones.

As always, consumer markets are all too eager to help us out of our predicament. Taking a hint from Stjepan Mestrovič,[37] Hargreaves suggests that 'emotions are extracted from this time-starved world of shrinking relationships and reinvested in consumable things. Advertising associates automobiles with passion and desire, and mobile telephones with inspiration and lust.' But however hard the merchants try, the hunger they promise to satiate won't go away. Humans have perhaps been recycled into consumables, but consumables cannot be made into humans. Not into the kinds of humans who inspire our desperate search for roots, kinship, friendship and love.

It needs to be admitted that consumable substitutes have an edge over the 'real stuff'. They promise freedom from the chores of endless negotiation and uneasy compromise; they swear to put paid to the vexing need for self-sacrifice, concessions, meeting others halfway that all intimate and loving bonds would sooner or later require. They come with an offer of losses being recuperated in case you find all such strains too heavy to bear. Their sellers vouch as well for an easy and frequent replacement of goods the moment you have no more use for them or other, new, improved and yet more seductive goods appear in sight. In short, consumables embody an ultimate non-finality and revocability of choices and an ultimate disposability of the objects chosen. More importantly yet, they seem to put us in control. It is we, the consumers, who draw the line between the useful and the waste. With consumables for partners, we can stop worrying about ending in the refuse bin.

Inadvertently, marketable consumables incarnate the ultimate paradox of the culture of waste:

First, it is the horrifying spectre of disposability – of redundancy, abandonment, rejection, exclusion, wastage – that sends us to seek security in a human embrace.

Second, it is from that expedition that we are diverted to the shopping malls.

Third, it is disposability itself, magically recycled from terminal disease into therapy, that we find there and are prompted to take home and store in first-aid boxes.

Comforted by our new knowledge, we sit down to watch – engrossed, enchanted, bewitched and transported – the next instalment of *Big Brother*, *The Weakest Link*, *Survivor* or whatever is the latest version of 'reality TV'. They all tell us the same story: that no one except a few solitary winners is truly indispensable, that a human is of use to other human beings only as long as she or he can be exploited to their advantage, that the waste bin, the ultimate destination of the excluded, is the natural prospect for those who no longer fit or no longer wish to be exploited in such a way, that survival is the name of the game of human togetherness and that the ultimate stake of survival is outliving the others. We are fascinated by what we see – just as Dali or De Chirico wished us to be fascinated by their canvases when they struggled to display the innermost, the hiddenmost contents of our subconscious fantasies and fears.

The older Big Brother, the one penned by George Orwell, presided over Fordist factories, military barracks and countless

other big and small panopticons of the Bentham/Foucault sort –
his sole wish was to keep our ancestors in and bring the stray sheep
back into the flock. The Big Brother of the TV 'reality shows' is
preoccupied solely with keeping odd men (and women) – the
unfit or less fit, the less clever or less zealous, the less endowed
and less resourceful – out; and once out, forever out.

The old Big Brother was preoccupied with *inclusion* – integra-
tion, getting people into line and keeping them there. The new
Big Brother's concern is *exclusion* – spotting the people who 'do
not fit' into the place they are in, banishing them from that place
and deporting them 'where they belong', or better still never
allowing them to come anywhere near in the first place. The new
Big Brother supplies the immigration officers with lists of people
they should not let in, and bankers with the list of people they
should not let into the company of the creditworthy. He instructs
the guards about whom they should stop at the gate and not let
inside the gated community. He inspires the neighbourhood-
watchers to spy out and kick out the suspected prowlers and loi-
terers – strangers out of place. He offers homeowners closed
circuit television to keep the undesirables away from the door. He
is the patron saint of all bouncers, whether in the service of a night
club or of a State Ministry of Home Affairs.

Of course, the news of the decease of the old-style Big Brother
is, as Mark Twain famously pointed out, grossly exaggerated. Both
Big Brothers – old and new – sit next to each other in the pass-
port control booths at airports, except that the new one scrupu-
lously checks travel documents on arrival whereas the old one
checks them, rather perfunctorily, on departure.

The old Big Brother is alive and better equipped than ever –
but now he is mostly to be found in the off-limits, marginalized
parts of social space such as urban ghettoes, refugee camps or
prisons. There, the old task remains of keeping people in and
bringing them in line whenever they fall out. As he was a hundred
years ago, that Big Brother is the patron saint of all varieties of
jailers. This is, you may say, an important role – and a role which,
because it is kept in the limelight and widely advertised, is commonly alleged to be even more important than it is. But it is now
a secondary, derivative, supplementary role to that played by the

new-style Big Brother; its true task is to make the new Big Brother's task a bit easier. Between themselves, the two brothers police and service the borderline between the 'inside' and the 'outside'. Their respective scopes work well together, depending on the sensitivity, porousness and vulnerability of borders.

Together, they embrace the whole of the social universe. You can move only from the sovereign realm of one Big Brother into the estate of the other – and one of the old-style Big Brother's functions is to make you see the vexing and repulsive attention of his younger sibling as a saving grace, a life-saving operation and a warrant of a secure and blissful existence. The inhuman cruelty of the first supports the devilish duplicity of the second. That is, as long as the only choice offered by the world we weave daily out of our life pursuits and in which our lives are woven is the choice between staying in line and rejection – between the warden-ships of the first or the second of the two Big Brothers jointly presiding over the game of obligatory inclusion and compulsory exclusion.

Throughout the last century, our ancestors fought back against the awesome powers of Big Brother, struggling to tear down the walls, barbed wire fences and watch-towers and dreaming of walking the paths of their own choice at the time of their own choice. They seem to have made much of their dream come true and so many of their descendants can manage to keep that Big Brother who watched them at a safe distance from the roads they walk – but only to fall under the watchful eye of Big Brother mark two. At the threshold of a new century the big question to which we, their descendants, will have to find an answer is whether the only choice open to humans is that between Big Brothers mark one and two: whether the inclusion/exclusion game is the only way in which human life in common may be conducted and the only conceivable form our shared world may take – be given – as a result.

Notes

Introduction

1 Italo Calvino, *Le città invisibili* (Einaudi, 1972), here quoted in William Weaver's translation, *Invisible Cities* (Vintage, 1997), pp. 67–8, 114–16.
2 Ivan Klima, *Láska a Smeti* (1986), here quoted in Ewald Osers' translation, *Love and Garbage* (Vintage, 2002), pp. 15–16.

1 In the beginning was design

Epigraph from Franz Kafka, 'Fellowship', in *The Collected Short Stories of Franz Kafka*, trans. Tania Stern and James Stern (Penguin, 1983).

1 See John Carvel, 'Depression on the rise among young', *Guardian*, 27 Nov. 2002.
2 Siegfried Kracauer, 'The group as bearer of ideas', in *Das Ornament der Masse* (1963), here quoted in Thomas Y. Levin's translation, *The Mass Ornament: Weimar Essays* (Harvard University Press, 1995), p. 143.
3 'Travel and dance', in *The Mass Ornament*, pp. 68–9.
4 Danièle Linhart, Barbara Rist and Estelle Durand, *Perte d'emploi, perte de soi* (Loss of work, loss of self) (Erès, 2002).
5 Danièle Linhart, 'Travail émietté, citoyens déboussolés', *Manière de Voir* 66 (Nov.–Dec. 2002), pp. 10–13.
6 Samuel Butler, *Erewhon* (Prometheus Books, 1998), p. 94.
7 'Funes, his memory', in Jorge Luis Borges, *Collected Fictions*, trans. Andrew Hurley (Penguin, 1998), pp. 129–37.
8 Milan Kundera, *Ignorance*, trans. Linda Asher (Faber, 2002), pp. 123–4.
9 'On exactitude in science', in Borges, *Collected Fictions*, p. 325.

10 Mary Douglas, *Purity and Danger: An Analysis of Concepts of Pollution and Taboo* (Penguin, 1970), p. 12.

11 Ibid., p. 49.

12 Kracauer, *The Mass Ornament*, p. 161.

13 Douglas, *Purity and Danger*, pp. 12 and 48.

14 Lewis Mumford, *The City in History: Its Origins, its Transformations, and its Prospects* (New York, 1961), pp. 450–1.

15 See Edmund R. Leach, 'Magical hair', in *Myth and Cosmos: Readings in Mythology and Symbolism*, ed. John Middleton (Natural History Press, 1967), pp. 77–108.

16 Tzvetan Todorov, *Devoirs et délices. Une vie de passeur* (interviews with Catherine Portevin) (Seuil, 2002), p. 304.

17 Tim Jordan, 'Technopower and its cyberfutures', in *Living with Cyberspace: Technology and Society in the Twenty-first Century*, ed. John Armitage and Joanne Roberts (Continuum, 2002), p. 125.

18 Geoffrey Bennington, *Interrupting Derrida* (Routledge, 2000), p. 164.

19 Giorgio Agamben, *Homo sacer. Il potere sovrano e la nuda vita* (1995), here quoted after Daniel Hellen–Roazen's translation, *Homo Sacer: Sovereign Power and Bare Life* (Stanford University Press, 1998), pp. 27, 18.

20 Ibid., p. 82.

21 Ibid., p. 83.

22 Giorgio Agamben, *Mezzi senza fine* (1996), here quoted after Vincenzo Binetti and Cesare Casarino's translation, *Means without Ends* (University of Minnesota Press, 2000), pp. 67–8.

2   Are there too many of them?

1 *Report of the TUC* (1883), p. 39.

2 J. B. Jeffreys, *Labour's Formative Years* (Lawrence and Wishart, 1948).

3 See Jacques Donzelot, Catherine Mével, Anne Wyvekens, 'De la fabrique sociale aux violences urbaines', *Esprit* (Dec. 2002), pp. 13–34.

4 See David Maybury-Lewis, 'Genocide against indigenous peoples', in *Annihilating Difference: The Anthropology of Genocide*, ed. Alexander Laban Hinton (University of California Press, 2002), pp. 43–53.

5 Quoted in Herman Merivale, *Lectures on Colonization and Colonies* (Green, Longman and Roberts, 1861), p. 541.

6 Theodore Roosevelt, *The Winning of the West: From the Alleghenies to the Mississipi, 1769–1776* (G. P. Putnam, 1889), p. 90.

7 According to Alfredo M. Serres Güliraldes, *La Estrategia de General Roca* (Pleamar, 1979), pp. 377–8, quoted in Merivale, *Lectures.*

8 See Chris McGreal, 'Bedouin feel the squeeze as Israel resettles the Negev desert', *Guardian*, 27 Feb. 2003, p. 19.

9 Stefan Czarnowski, 'Ludzie zbędni w słuźbie przemocy' (Redundant people in the service of violence) (1935), in *Dziela*, vol. 2 (PWN, 1956), pp. 186–93.

10 Hauke Brunkhorst, 'Global society as the crisis of democracy', in *The Transformation of Modernity: Aspects of the Past, Present and Future of an Era*, ed. Mikael Carleheden and Michael Hviid Jacobsen (Ashgate, 2001), p. 233.

11 Richard Rorty, 'Failed prophecies, glorious hopes', in *Philosophy and Social Hope* (Penguin, 1999), p. 203.

12 See Mikhail Bakhtin, *Rabelais and his World* (MIT Press, 1968) translated from the Russian edition of 1965. Also Ken Hirschkop's apt summary in 'Fear and democracy: an essay on Bakhtin's theory of carnival', *Associations* 1 (1997), pp. 209–34.

13 See 'The Burrow', in *The Collected Short Stories of Franz Kafka*, ed. Naum N. Glatzer (Penguin, 1988), pp. 325–59.

14 Siegfried Kracauer, 'Franz Kafka: on his posthumous works', in *Das Ornament der Masse* (1963), here quoted after Thomas Y. Levin's translation, *The Mass Ornament: Weimar Essays* (Harvard University Press, 1995, p. 268).

15 See Robert Castel, *Métamorphoses de la question sociale. Une chronique du salariat* (Fayard, 1995).

16 See Ulrich Beck, *Risiko Gesellschaft. Auf dem Weg in einere andere Moderne* (Suhrkamp, 1986), here quoted after Mark Ritter's translation *Risk Society* (Sage, 1992), p.137.

17 See Anna More, 'Raising a false alarm', *Observer Magazine*, 26 Jan. 2003, pp. 85–6.

18 See Stephen Castles, 'Towards a sociology of forced migration and social transformation', *Sociology* 1 (2003), pp. 13–34.

19 Philippe Robert and Laurent Mucchielli, *Crime et insécurité. L'état de savoirs* (La Découverte, 2002). See also 'Une généalogie de l'insécurité contemporaine. Entretien avec Philippe Robert', *Esprit* (Dec. 2002), pp. 35–58.

20 Hans-Jörg Albrecht, 'Immigration, crime and safety', in *Crime and Insecurity: The Governance of Safety in Europe*, ed. Adam Crawford (Willan, 2002), pp. 159–85.

21 Adam Crawford, 'The governance of crime and insecurity in an anxious age: the trans-European and the local', in ibid., p. 32.

22 Leon Zedner, 'The pursuit of security', in *Crime, Risk and Insecurity*, ed. T. Hope and R. Sparks (Routledge, 2000), p. 201.

23 Meaning, roughly, that if A comes before B (or coincides with B) this does not prove that A and B are related as cause and effect.

24 Jelle van Buuren, 'Le droit d'asile refoulé à la frontière', *Manière de Voir*, Mar.–Apr. 2002, pp. 76–80.

25 Rachel Shabi, 'The e-waste land', *Guardian Weekend*, 30 Nov. 2002, pp. 36–9.

26 Naomi Klein, 'Fortress continents', *Guardian*, 16 Jan. 2003, p. 23. The article was first published in the *Nation*.

3 To each waste its dumping site

1 See François de Bernard, *La Pauvreté durable* (Felin, 2002), pp. 37–9.

2 Richard Rorty, 'Globalization, the politics of identity and social hope', in *Philosophy and Social Hope* (Penguin, 1999), pp. 229–39.

3 'Des Königs viele Lieber. Die Selbstdekonstruktion der Hierarchie des Rechts', *Soziale Systeme* 2 (1996); E.-W. Böckenförde, *Staat, Verfassung, Demokratie* (Suhrkamp, 1991).

4 Hauke Brunkhorst, 'Global society as the crisis of democracy', in *The Transformation of Modernity* (Ashgate, 2001), p. 236.

5 See Zygmunt Bauman, *Society under Siege* (Polity, 2002).

6 Stewart Hall, 'Out of a clear blue sky', *Soundings* (winter 2001–2), pp. 9–15.

7 David Garland, *The Culture of Control: Crime and Social Order in Contemporary Society* (Oxford University Press, 2001), p. 175.

8 Loïc Wacquant, 'Comment la "tolérance zéro" vint à l'Europe', *Manière de Voir* (Mar.–Apr. 2001), pp. 38–46.

9 See Peter Andreas and Timothy Snyder, *The Wall around the West* (Rowman and Littlefield, 2000).

10 Ulf Hedetoft, *The Global Turn: National Encounters with the World* (Aalborg University Press, 2003), pp. 151–2.

11 Rosa Luxemburg, *The Accumulation of Capital*, trans. Agnes Schwarzschild (Routledge, 1961), pp. 387, 416.

12 At the time of the Gulf War, 'when Saddam turned his helicopter gunships on the Iraqi Kurds, they tried to flee north over the mountains into Turkey – but the Turks refused to let them in. They physically whipped them back at the border crossings. I heard one

Turkish officer say. "We hate these people. They're fucking pigs." So for weeks the Kurds were stuck in the mountains at 10 below zero, often with only the clothes they were wearing when they fled. The children suffered the most: dysentery, typhoid, malnutrition . . .', see Maggie O'Kane, 'The most pitiful sights I have ever seen', *Guardian*, 14 Feb. 2003, pp. 6–11.

13 Garry Younge, 'A world full of strangers', *Soundings* (winter 2001–2), pp. 18–22.

14 See Alan Travis, 'Treatment of asylum seekers "is inhumane"', *Guardian*, 11 Feb. 2003, p. 7.

15 See Alan Travis, 'Blunkett to fight asylum ruling', *Guardian*, 20 Feb. 2003, p. 2.

16 See Michel Agier, *Aux bords du monde, les réfugiés* (Flammarion, 2002), pp. 55–6.

17 Ibid., p. 86.

18 Ibid., p. 94.

19 Ibid., p. 117.

20 Ibid., p. 120.

21 See Sharon Stenton Russell, 'Refugees: risks and challenges worldwide', *Migration Information Source*, 26 Nov. 2002.

22 See Fabienine Rose Émilie le Houerou, 'Camps de la soif au Soudan', *Le Monde Diplomatique*, May 2003, p. 28.

23 See Loïc Wacquant, 'Urban outcasts: stigma and division in the black American ghetto and the French urban periphery', *International Journal of Urban and Regional Research* 3 (1993), pp. 365–83; 'A black city within the white: revising America's black ghetto', *Black Renaissance* (fall/winter 1998), pp. 142–51.

24 See Loïc Wacquant, 'Deadly symbiosis: when ghetto and prison meet and mesh', *Punishment and Society* 1 (2002), pp. 95–134.

25 Jerome G. Miller, *Search and Destroy: African-American Males in the Criminal Justice System* (Cambridge University Press, 1997), p. 101.

26 Wacquant, 'Deadly symbiosis'.

27 See 'Une généalogie de l'insécurité contemporaine', entretien avec Philippe Robert, *Esprit* (Dec. 2002), pp. 35–58.

28 See Hughes Lagrange and Thierry Pech, 'Délinquance: les rendezvous de l'état social', *Esprit* (Dec. 2002), pp. 71–85.

29 Wacquant 'Comment la "tolérance zéro" vint à l'Europe', p. 40.

30 See Henry A. Giroux, 'Global capitalism and the return of the garrison state', *Arena Journal* 19 (2002), pp. 141–60.

31 Garland, *The Culture of Control*, pp. 177–8.

32 Ibid., p. 180.

33 Ibid., pp. 184–5.
34 Ibid., p. 178.

4 Culture of waste

1   See Jorge Luis Borges, *Collected Fictions*, trans. Andrew Hurley (Penguin, 1998), pp. 183–95.
2   Hans Jonas, 'The burden and blessing of mortality', *Hasting Center Report* 1 (1992), pp. 34–40.
3   Ernest Becker, *The Denial of Death* (Free Press, 1973), p. 7.
4   Ibid., pp. 7, 4, 5.
5   See the chapter 'Diversions' in *Pensées*, trans. A. J. Krailsheimer (Penguin, 1966), pp. 66–72.
6   Max Scheler, *Tod und Fortleben*, here quoted after Polish translation by Adam Wegrzecki, *Cierpienie, Smierc, Dalsze Zycie* (PWN, 1993).
7   George Steiner, *Errata: An Examined Life* (Phoenix, 1998), p. 85.
8   Quotes from *The Brothers Karamazov* in my translation, following a 1970 edition (Karelskoe Knizhnoe Izdatelstvo, Petrozavodsk), pp. 78ff, 636, 702–3.
9   Larry Jay Young, *Diminished Being* (Oslo University College, 2002), pp. 159ff.
10 For here and below, see Conal Walsh, 'Fallen idols of the free market', *Observer*, 26 July 2002, pp. 8–9.
11 Here and below, report by Erik Baard, *Village Voice*, 22–8 Jan. 2003, quoted after the *Guardian*, 8 Feb. 2003.
12 Oliver Burkman, 'My dad is a living deterrent...' *Guardian*, 21 Mar. 2001.
13 Richard Sennett, *The Corrosion of Character* (Norton, 1998), p. 25.
14 John Kotter, *The New Rules* (Dutton, 1995), p. 159.
15 See the report by Ben Summerskill and Tom Reilly in the *Observer*, 19 Jan. 2003, p. 13.
16 See Frédéric F. Clairmont, 'Vivre à crédit ou le credo de la première puissance du monde', *Le Monde Diplomatique*, Apr. 2003, pp. 20–1.
17 See Michelle Ogundehin, 'California dreams', *Observer Magazine*, 12 Jan. 2003, pp. 36–7.
18 See Caroline Roux, 'To die for', *Guardian Weekend*, 1 Feb. 2003.
19 See Peter Paphides, 'Seven inches of heaven', *Guardian Weekend*, 16 Nov. 2002, pp. 54ff.
20 See my *Society under Siege* (Polity, 2002), ch. 4.

21   See Alberto Melucci, *The Playing Self: Person and Meaning in the Planetary Society* (Cambridge University Press, 1996), pp. 43ff. This is an extended version of the Italian original published in 1991 under the title *Il gioco dell'io.*

22   See Randeep Ramesh, 'The two faces of Rumsfeld', *Guardian*, 9 May 2003, p. 1.

23   Yves Michaud, *L'art à l'état gazeux. Essai sur la triomphe de l'esthé-tique* (Stock, 2003), pp. 7, 9, 77, 120–1.

24   S. Daney, *La salaire du zappeur* (POL, 1993), p. 12.

25   Sigmund Freud, *Civilization, Society and Religion*, vol. 12 of The Pelican Freud Library (Penguin, 1991), pp. 271, 281, 282.

26   Here and below, see Hugh Wilson, 'This year's love', *Observer Magazine*, 10 Nov. 2002, pp. 74–5.

27   See Ray Pahl, *On Friendship* (Polity, 2000).

28   See Anushka Asthana, 'I have only three minutes to get to know the love of my life', *Observer*, 26 Jan. 2003, p. 9.

29   Emma Taylor and Lorelei Sharkey, 'Personal ads are for lonely hearts', *Guardian Weekend*, 19 Apr. 2003, p. 50.

30   Barbara Ellen, 'Being in a relationship is like being at the office . . .', *Observer Magazine*, 20 Apr. 2003, p. 7.

31   See Oliver James, 'Constant craving', *Observer Magazine*, 19 Jan. 2003, p. 71.

32   See 'Taking a stand', *Observer Magazine*, 19 Jan. 2003, p. 73.

33   See Richard Sennett, 'Flexibilité sur la ville', *Manière de Voir* (Nov.–Dec. 2002), pp. 59–63.

34   Charles Handy, *The Elephant and the Flea* (Hutchinson, 2001), p. 204.

35   Andy Hargreaves, *Teaching in the Knowledge Society: Education in the Age of Insecurity* (Open University Press, 2003), p. 25.

36   Clifford Stoll, *Silicon Snakeoil* (Doubleday, 1995), p. 58.

37   Stjepan Mestrovič, *Postemotional Society* (Sage, 1997).